Home Court Advantage

JUNIOR SERVICE LEAGUE OF WOODSTOCK

DELICIOUS RECIPES FOR CASUAL ENTERTAINING

MW0090105

Home Court Advantage
DELICIOUS RECIPES FOR CASUAL ENTERTAINING

Copyright 2000 by The Junior Service League of Woodstock

The Junior Service League of Woodstock is an organization of women committed to promoting volunteerism and to improving the community through the effective action and leadership of trained volunteers. Its purpose is exclusively educational and charitable.

The profit realized by the Junior Service League of Woodstock from the sale of *Home Court Advantage* will be used for projects it sponsors in the community.

The Junior Service League of Woodstock would like to thank our illustrator, Julia Mahood and our elementary school artists for all of their creative ingredients which helped give *Home Court Advantage* its own unique flavor.

1st printing   October 2000

ISBN: 0-9701693-0-2
LCCCN: 00 192072

Printed in the USA by

WIMMER
The Wimmer Companies
Memphis
1-800-548-2537

of Woodstock

Introduction

We're not sure who first coined the phrase "Hey, let's put together a cookbook!", but it's one that every Service League has heard at one time or another. At first this seems like a fairly simple task, but once the water starts to boil (so to speak) it becomes countless hours of collecting recipes, deciding what kind of book you want, testing recipes, working with designers and publishers, and oh yes, tasting recipes. There's a lot of work that goes into making the idea of a cookbook a reality.

As the Junior Service League of Woodstock proudly celebrates its tenth year of volunteerism, we are also pleased to introduce our cookbook *Home Court Advantage*. We hope you enjoy using this cookbook and share the recipes with friends and loved ones. It's so nice to be at a gathering and hear "Who made this great dish and where can I get the recipe?". There is no greater compliment than to have the response be, "I've got this great little cookbook called *Home Court Advantage*." Bon Appetit!

Contributor's List

Home Court Advantage is a collection of over 200 recipes whose compilation would not have been possible without the cooperation of our membership. The cookbook committee wishes to express sincere appreciation to the contributors, testers and tasters for their assistance and support.

Donna Aber	Kelli Coerver	Rebecca Hayes	Megan McNairy*
Alyssa Allen	Laura Commanday*	Jennifer Hillhouse	Kathy McNamara
Michele Allison*	Elaine Cozart*	Vickie Howland	Cindy Miller*
Becky Anderson	Joannie Crotts*	Linda Peery Hunt*	Jenny Mummert
Amanda Arnold	Colleen Crumpton	Lori Hunter*	LeAnna Mutchler
Andrea Back*	Sara Ann Curson	Trisha Hunter	Janet O'Brien
Karen Baird	Sydney Dahlman	Trina Hutchison	Kim Owen
Gretchen Beach*	Sherry D'Ambrosio	Kelly Ingram	Tammy Padgett
Sandy Bessenger*	Deannie de la Guardia*	Valerie Johnson	Kitty Peecher*
Stephanie Betts	Andrea Debranski	Cindy Jones*	Theresa Peltier
Leigh Birdsong	Maggie DeCan	Candy Jordan	Kathy Pinson
Debby Bishop	Sabrina Dobbs	Deanna King	Sherry Pittman*
Deanna Boling	Jean Elliot	Denise La Haye	Patti Quagliaroli
Melissa Booth	Lynn Favre	Bria Lott	Kathleen Ratliff*
Christine Boraks	Beth Ferguson	Julie Loren	Michelle Renn
Mary Bowerman	Jean Foley	Regina Mabrey	Becky Robertson
Page Burklow*	Teri Gentry	Mary Kal Macken	Jackie Ross
Kelly Burleson	Gail George	Ginny Manning	Lisa Sams
Janet Carver	Roxanne Griffen	Hope Martin	Donna Sanders
Donna Charriat	Melinda Gulick	Michelle Daniel	Kelley Sangery
Beth Choppa	Kim Hagood	Lisa Mason*	Barbara Sansing
Robin Clayton	Robin Hall	Lorie McDaniel	Kim Schlefflebein

Cathy Schmidt	Tricia Skalak
Linda Siebold	Ann Smith
Trisha Sievers	Michele Smith
Colleen Simon*	Theresa Tardell
	DeAnn Taylor
	Vildan Teske
	Pam Tinsley
	Brandie Unterreiner
	Pat Walker*
	Betsy Ward
	Ginger Williams
	Gwen Williams
	Tami Williams
	Candace Youngberg*
	Andrea Zampatti
	Julie Zaner*
	Amy Zierow*

COOKBOOK CHAIRPERSONS: Sandy Bessenger and Lisa Mason, 1998–2000

SPECIAL CONTRIBUTOR: Chef Andrew Featherstone

Note: "" indicates Cookbook Committee Member*

Student Art Contest Grand Prize Winner

Cindy, grade 4 • Little River Elementary

Fun and Games: Casual Entertaining Menus

Rodney, grade 4 • Oak Grove Elementary

Suggested Menus

WEEKEND BREAKFAST
Stuffed French Toast, p. 104
Bacon or Sausage
Fresh Seasonal Fruit
Marshmallow Fruit Dip, p. 36
Fresh Juices / Milk

HOLIDAY BRUNCH
Weekend Breakfast Casserole. p. 107
Cheese Grits, p. 110
Fresh Seasonal Fruit
Melissa's Blue Ribbon Orange Bread, p. 55
Mimosas

COURTSIDE CUISINE
Fresh Orange Juice
Sour Cream Muffins, p. 55
Mini Sausage Melts, p. 109
Baked Ham and Cheese Rolls, p. 25
Tennis Time Broccoli Salad, p. 81
Or
Oriental Cole Slaw, p. 79
Fresh Seasonal Fruit
Black Bean Salsa with Tortilla Chips, p.35
Neiman Marcus Cookies, p. 124
Or
Cream Cheese Brownies, p. 135
Frozen Margarita Punch, p. 174

CARDS & DICE

Sweet Vidalia Onion Dip, p. 13
Club Spinach Dip, p. 15
Thai Chicken on a Skewer with
    Peanut Sauce, p. 97
Cocktail Reubens, p. 23
Mexican Rollups, p. 23
Chile Con Queso Dip and Tortilla Chips, p. 19
Cherry Cheese Cake Bars, p. 129
Pecan Tassies, p. 139

BIG GAME FARE

Mini Potato Skins, p. 21
Barbecued Water Chestnuts, p. 21
Southern Stuffed Mushrooms, p. 45
Nuts & Bolts, p. 44
Sassy Saucy Meatballs, p. 27
Snickers Brownies, p. 133
Beer & Wine

SUMMER SUPPER CLUB

Crab Stuffed Mushrooms, p. 46
Garlic Tenderloin, p. 100
Ultimate Greek Salad, p. 73
Corn on the Cob
Easy Key Lime Pie, p. 143
Summer Sangria, p. 171

RAINING BRIDES AND BABIES

Tutti Fruity Punch, p. 169
Curry Chicken Salad, p. 87
Towne Lake Tortellini Salad, p. 86
Strawberry Pretzel Salad, p. 118
Yeast Rolls
Italian Cream Cake, p. 151

FIRESIDE DINNER

El Presidente's Salsa and Tortilla Chips, p. 35
Woodstock Waldorf, p. 85
White Chili, p. 69
Broccoli Corn Bread, p. 63
Toffee Brownie Bars, p. 132

Serve and Volley: Warm Up with Appetizers and Snacks

Sweet Vidalia Onion Dip

2	cups chopped Vidalia onion, or other sweet onion in season	¼	teaspoon garlic salt
2	cups shredded Swiss cheese	¼	teaspoon celery salt
2	cups mayonnaise		

Preheat oven to 350°. In a medium bowl, mix onion, cheese, mayonnaise, garlic salt and celery salt until well blended. Pour mixture into a 2 quart baking dish. Bake at 350° for 30 to 40 minutes or until golden and slightly bubbling. Stir before serving. Serve with your favorite corn chips or crackers.

Yield: 8 to 12 servings

Spinach Dip Olé

1	(10 ounce) package frozen chopped spinach, thawed and squeezed dry	1	(8 ounce) package cream cheese, cubed
1	(16 ounce) jar medium or hot salsa	2	cups shredded Monterey Jack cheese
2	(4½ ounce) cans sliced black olives	1	tablespoon red wine vinegar
			Salt and pepper to taste

Preheat oven to 400°. Combine spinach, salsa, olives, cheeses, vinegar, salt and pepper in a large bowl. Mix well and pour into a shallow baking dish. Bake at 400° for 25 minutes or until bubbly and brown on top. Serve with tortilla chips or large corn chips.

Yield: 8 servings

Kentucky Green Grass

1	medium onion, chopped	2	(6 ounce) cans crabmeat
2	sticks butter	1½	cups Parmesan cheese
2	(10 ounce) packages frozen spinach, thawed and squeezed dry		

Sauté onion in butter in a large skillet. Stir in spinach, crabmeat and cheese and cook until heated through. Serve warm, preferably in a chafing dish or fondue pot, with pita or nacho chips.

Yield: 12 servings

Herb Pita Pieces

8	pita bread rounds	1	teaspoon dried basil
2	sticks butter, melted	1	teaspoon dried parsley
1	teaspoon dried oregano	2	cloves garlic, minced
1	teaspoon dried marjoram		

Preheat oven to 300°. Separate pita bread so each forms two thin rounds. Break pita rounds into cracker-size pieces. Combine butter, oregano, marjoram, basil, parsley and garlic in a small bowl. Brush pita pieces with butter mixture and place on a baking sheet. Bake at 300° for 30 minutes or to desired crispness. Serve with hot or cold dips.

Yield: about 5 dozen

Club Spinach Dip

1	(8 ounce) package cream cheese, cubed	6	slices bacon, cooked and crumbled
⅓	cup Parmesan cheese	1	(10 ounce) frozen spinach, thawed and squeezed dry
½	cup mayonnaise	1	teaspoon lemon juice
2-4	green onions, chopped		

Preheat oven to 350°. Combine cheeses, mayonnaise, onion, bacon, spinach and lemon juice. Transfer to a shallow baking dish and bake at 350° for 15 minutes. Serve hot or warm with crackers or veggies.

Yield: 6 servings

Greek Spinach Dip

1	tablespoon diced onion	2	cups shredded mozzarella cheese
	Olive oil for sautéing	1	(10 ounce) can diced tomatoes and green chiles
8	ounces feta cheese	1	(10 ounce) package frozen spinach, thawed and squeezed dry

Preheat oven to 350°. Sauté onion in olive oil. Combine sautéed onion, cheeses, tomatoes and chiles and spinach in a mixing bowl. Mix until well blended. Spread mixture in a casserole dish and bake at 350° until melted. Serve with pita chips.

Yield: 8 servings

To make pita chips, cut pita bread into chip-size pieces. Brush with olive oil and bake at 350° until crispy.

Mix and Match Artichoke Dip

1	(14 ounce) can artichoke hearts, drained and chopped	¼	teaspoon Worcestershire sauce
¾	cup mayonnaise or mayonnaise-type salad dressing	2-3	drops hot pepper sauce
1	clove garlic, minced		

Preheat oven to 350°. Combine artichoke hearts, mayonnaise, garlic, Worcestershire sauce and hot pepper sauce in a large mixing bowl. Transfer to a lightly greased 1 quart casserole dish. Bake at 350° for 20 minutes or until bubbly. Serve with Melba toast rounds or crackers.

Yield: 8 servings

For variety, try adding any one of the following before baking:

1. 1 (10 ounce) package frozen chopped spinach
2. 1 (4 ounce) can sliced green chiles
3. 2 cups cooked chopped chicken
4. 1 cup grated Parmesan cheese

Spinach and Artichoke Dip

1   (8 ounce) package cream cheese, cubed
4   ounces Swiss cheese, shredded
2   ounces grated Parmesan cheese
½   cup mayonnaise

¼   (1 ounce) packet dry Italian dressing mix
1   (10 ounce) package frozen chopped spinach, thawed and squeezed dry
1   (6 ounce) can artichokes, drained and chopped

Preheat oven to 325°. Combine cheeses, mayonnaise and dry dressing mix in a mixing bowl. Stir in spinach and artichokes. Transfer to a shallow baking dish and bake at 325° for 20 minutes. Serve with warm tortilla chips.

Yield: 12 servings

Pizza Dip

1   (8 ounce) package cream cheese
1   (14 ounce) jar pizza sauce
⅓   cup chopped onion

1½ cups shredded mozzarella cheese
1   (6 ounce) can black olives, drained and chopped
2   ounces pepperoni slices

Preheat oven to 350°. Press cream cheese into bottom of a 9 inch glass pie pan. Spread pizza sauce over cream cheese. Layer onion, mozzarella cheese, olives and pepperoni on sauce. Bake at 350° for 25 minutes. Serve with light corn chips.

Yield: 8 servings

Nacho Dip

1	(8 ounce) can refried beans or bean dip	1	(8 ounce) package shredded Colby Jack cheese
1	(8 ounce) jar picante sauce		

Preheat oven to 350°. Spread beans in bottom of an 8 or 9 inch pie pan. Spread picante sauce over beans. Sprinkle cheese over sauce. Bake at 350° for 10 minutes or microwave for 10 minutes or until cheese is melted. Serve with tortilla chips.

Yield: 8 servings

For variety, add a layer of sour cream (8 ounce container) before adding cheese. Vary recipe further by adding chopped green chiles to taste.

Chili Dip

1	pound ground beef	1	(6 ounce) can tomato paste
1	cup chopped onion	1½	cups water
1	(1¼ ounce) envelope dry chili seasoning	1	(8 ounce) package cream cheese, cubed

Brown beef and onions; drain. Add chili seasoning, tomato paste and water. Stir until mixed. Simmer 10 minutes. Add cream cheese and stir until melted, being careful to prevent burning. Serve with corn or tortilla chips.

Yield: 8 to 12 servings

Chile Con Queso Dip

1 pound bulk sausage, mild, medium or hot
1 pound Velveeta cheese, diced or shredded
1 pound Monterey Jack cheese, diced or shredded
2 (10 ounce) cans diced tomatoes and green chiles

Brown sausage; drain. In a glass bowl, melt cheeses in a microwave, stir until smooth. Stir melted cheeses and tomatoes and chiles into sausage. Serve warm in a crock pot with tortilla chips.

Yield: 20 servings

Hot Broccoli Dip

1 medium onion, finely chopped
1 (4 ounce) can mushroom stems and pieces, drained
1 tablespoon butter
1 cup shredded sharp cheddar cheese
1 tablespoon garlic powder
1 (10¾ ounce) can condensed cream of mushroom soup
2 (10 ounce) packages broccoli, cooked, drained and chopped
Dash of Worcestershire sauce
Dash of hot pepper sauce
Dash of cayenne pepper
Salt to taste

Sauté onion and mushrooms in butter in a saucepan. In a double boiler, melt cheese. Add sautéed vegetables, garlic powder, soup, broccoli, Worcestershire sauce, hot pepper sauce, cayenne pepper and salt to double boiler. Stir well. Serve warm in a chafing dish with corn chips.

Yield: 8 servings

Tennessee Sin

2	(16 ounce) loaves French bread, unsliced, divided	1/3	cup chopped green onions	
1	(8 ounce) package cream cheese, softened	1/3	cup chopped green bell pepper	
1	(8 ounce) container sour cream	1/4	teaspoon Worcestershire sauce	
2	cups shredded cheddar cheese		Paprika	
1/2	cup chopped cooked ham			

Preheat oven to 350°. Slice off top fourth of 1 loaf of bread. Hollow out the bottom half, leaving a 1 inch shell. Cut top half and remaining loaf into 1 inch cubes and place on a large baking sheet. Bake cubes at 350° for about 12 minutes or until lightly browned. In a medium mixing bowl, beat cream cheese with an electric mixer on medium speed until smooth. Add sour cream and beat until creamy. Stir in cheddar cheese, ham, onions, bell pepper and Worcestershire sauce. Spoon into bread shell, wrap in heavy-duty foil and place on a baking sheet. Bake at 350° for 30 minutes. Unwrap and place on a serving platter. Sprinkle with paprika. Serve with toasted bread cubes or corn chips.

Yield: 12 servings

Mini Potato Skins

1 (2 pound) package frozen shredded hash browns, thawed
1 egg, beaten
1½ cups shredded cheddar cheese

⅓ cup chopped cooked bacon
½ cup sour cream
Salt and pepper to taste

Preheat oven to 400°. Combine hash browns and egg. Place mixture in greased mini or regular muffin tins. Bake at 400° for 30 minutes. Sprinkle tops with cheese and bacon. Return to oven and bake 3 minutes longer or until cheese is melted. Top with sour cream. Season with salt and pepper.

Yield: 24 to 48 servings

Barbecued Water Chestnuts

2 (8 ounce) cans whole water chestnuts, drained
1 pound bacon, slices cut into thirds
1 cup brown sugar

1 teaspoon soy sauce
1 cup ketchup

Preheat oven to 375°. Wrap each chestnut with a bacon slice and fasten with a toothpick. Place wrapped chestnuts in a 9x13 inch pan and bake at 375° for 45 minutes. Drain fat. Combine brown sugar, soy sauce and ketchup. Pour mixture over chestnuts and bake 35 minutes longer.

Yield: 10 to 15 servings

Spanish olives

1	**(8 ounce) package cream cheese, softened**	**1**	**cup chopped pecans**
1	**(10 ounce) jar large or jumbo pimento-stuffed Spanish olives, drained and patted dry**		

Mold a small dollop of cream cheese around each olive. When all olives are completely covered by cheese, roll each olive in pecans. Layer in an airtight container between wax paper. Refrigerate for up to 3 days. Cut olives in half before serving.

Yield: about 48 pieces

Do not substitute Neufchâtel cheese or fat-free cream cheese.

Saucy Sausage

2	**pounds smoked sausage, sliced ¼-inch thick, or cocktail wieners**	**1**	**(12 ounce) jar chili sauce**
3	**cups apple juice**	**1**	**(10 ounce) jar currant jelly**

Combine sausage slices or wieners and apple juice in a saucepan. Bring to a simmer and cook 20 minutes. Drain sausage, discarding juice. Combine chili sauce and jelly in saucepan and mix until smooth. Add sausage and toss until coated. Serve in a warming tray.

Yield: about 100 pieces

Cocktail Reubens

½   pound thinly sliced corned beef, chopped
1   (14 ounce) can sauerkraut, drained
1   cup Thousand Island salad dressing

1   cup shredded Swiss cheese
1   regular loaf rye bread or 2 packages party rye bread

Preheat oven to 375°. In a medium bowl, combine beef, sauerkraut, dressing and cheese. Mix well. If using a regular loaf of bread, cut each slice into square quarters. Arrange half the bread quarters or party slices on a baking sheet. Spread slices with beef mixture. Top with remaining bread slices to make mini sandwiches. Bake at 375° for 10 to 12 minutes.

Yield: 40 mini sandwiches

Mexican Rollups

1   (8 ounce) package cream cheese
2   cups shredded sharp cheddar cheese
1   (4 ounce) can diced jalapeño peppers or green chiles, drained

⅓   cup chopped black olives
6   (8 inch) flour tortillas
   Salsa

Blend cheeses. Add peppers and olives. Spread mixture evenly over tortillas. Roll up tortillas and wrap individually in plastic wrap. Chill 3 hours. Cut each tortilla roll diagonally into 10 slices. Serve with salsa.

Yield: 6 servings

Chicken and Broccoli Twist

2	(8 ounce) packages refrigerated crescent roll dough		½	cup mayonnaise
2	cups chopped cooked chicken		1	teaspoon dried dill weed
1	cup chopped broccoli		¼	teaspoon salt
½	cup chopped red bell pepper		1	egg white, beaten
1	cup shredded sharp cheddar cheese		2	tablespoons slivered almonds
1	clove garlic, pressed			

Preheat oven to 375°. Press dough into one long rectangle on an ungreased baking sheet. Cut 1½ inch strips from the long sides of the rectangle to the center, leaving 3 inches in the center uncut. Blend chicken, broccoli, bell pepper, cheese, garlic, mayonnaise, dill weed and salt. Pour mixture onto middle 3 inches of dough. Twist each strip and fold over mixture. Brush twisted dough with egg white. Sprinkle almonds on top. Bake at 375° for 25 to 28 minutes. Slice and serve.

Yield: 10 servings

Baked Ham and Cheese Rolls

2	sticks margarine, softened
2	tablespoons poppy seeds
3-4	tablespoons yellow mustard
1	small onion, finely chopped
1	tablespoon Worcestershire sauce

	Salt and pepper to taste
3	(12 ounce) packages Pepperidge Farm soft country-style dinner rolls
1	pound baked ham, thinly sliced
2	cups shredded Swiss cheese

Preheat oven to 250°. Combine margarine, poppy seeds, mustard, onion, Worcestershire sauce, salt and pepper in a small bowl. Slice rolls in half horizontally. Spread margarine mixture over cut sides of rolls. Divide ham and cheese among bottom halves of rolls. Firmly press on top half of each roll. Wrap sandwiches, 12 at a time, in foil packages. Bake at 250° for 10 minutes or until cheese is melted.

Yield: 36 sandwiches

Sandwiches can be refrigerated or frozen before baking. After sandwiches are prepared, wrap in plastic. To bake the next day, refrigerate over night (this also allows flavors time to blend). Remove from refrigerator 30 minutes before baking and bake in foil as directed above. If freezing sandwiches, thaw sandwiches before baking as directed above for 10 to 20 minutes or until cheese melts.

Party Bread

1	pound hot sausage	1/2	teaspoon garlic salt
1	pound ground beef	1	teaspoon oregano
1	pound Velveeta cheese, cubed or shredded	1	loaf party rye bread
1/2	teaspoon Worcestershire sauce		

Preheat oven to 400°. Brown sausage and ground beef in a skillet. Drain well and return to skillet. Add cheese and heat until cheese is melted. Add Worcestershire sauce, garlic salt and oregano. Spread mixture generously on bread slices. Bake at 400° for about 15 minutes.

Yield: 12 servings

Sausage Bites

1	pound mild or spicy sausage	8	ounces Monterey Jack cheese, shredded
1	medium onion, chopped	1/2	teaspoon oregano
1	red bell pepper, chopped		Salt and pepper
2	teaspoons olive oil	3	packages frozen mini phyllo shells

Brown sausage, onion and bell pepper in oil. Drain well and cool to room temperature. Add cheese, oregano, salt and pepper. Mix well. Spoon into phyllo shells. Bake at 350° for 5 minutes or until hot.

Yield: 3 to 4 dozen

Sassy Saucy Meatballs

MEATBALLS

2	slices bread		3	tablespoons fresh parsley, or 1 tablespoon dried
¼	cup milk		3	tablespoons Parmesan cheese
1½	pounds ground beef round		½	teaspoon salt
1	egg, beaten		1	teaspoon black pepper
1	teaspoon oregano			

SAUCE

1	envelope dry onion soup mix		2	tablespoons brown sugar
1	(16 ounce) can jellied cranberry sauce		2	tablespoons lemon juice
12	ounces chili sauce			

Preheat oven to 350°. Soak bread slices in milk; set aside. Combine ground beef, egg, oregano, parsley, cheese, salt and pepper. Add bread mixture and stir well. Shape into small meatballs and place on a foil-lined baking sheet. Bake at 350° for 30 to 45 minutes, checking after 25 minutes. Drain on paper towels.

To make sauce, combine soup mix, cranberry sauce, chili sauce, brown sugar and lemon juice in a saucepan. Cook until heated. To serve, place cooked meatballs in a crock pot or chafing dish and pour sauce over the meatballs. Serve warm.

Yield: 25 to 30 servings

Baked Brie

1	stick butter	1/4	teaspoon ground nutmeg	
1/2	cup brown sugar	1	(12 ounce) wheel Brie cheese	
1/2	cup granulated sugar	2	tablespoons sliced almonds, toasted	
1/2	cup heavy cream	1	French baguette, sliced	

Preheat oven to 225°. Combine butter and sugars in a medium saucepan. Cook over low heat until butter is melted and sugar is dissolved. Remove from heat and add cream. Beat mixture until thickened. Add nutmeg. Return to low heat and stir until mixture is caramelized but still thick. Pour mixture over cheese in an oven-safe dish or pie plate. Bake at 225° for 10 minutes. Garnish with almonds. Serve with baguette slices.

Yield: 6 servings

Jarlsberg Cheese Dip

8	ounces Jarlsberg cheese, shredded	1/2	onion, grated or finely chopped
1	cup mayonnaise		Black pepper to taste

Preheat oven to 350°. Combine cheese, mayonnaise, onion and pepper in an oven-safe dish. Bake at 350° for 20 to 30 minutes. Serve with pita chips, bagel chips or bread sticks.

Yield: 8 servings

Marinated Cheese

1	(8 ounce) block sharp cheddar cheese		½	cup white wine vinegar
1	(8 ounce) package cream cheese		1	(2 ounce) jar diced pimento, drained
1	teaspoon sugar		3	tablespoons chopped fresh parsley
¾	teaspoon dried basil		3	tablespoons minced green onion
	Dash of salt		3	cloves garlic, pressed
	Dash of black pepper			Fresh parsley sprigs
½	cup olive oil			

Cut cheeses into ¼ inch slices, then cut slices in half. Arrange cheese in a small dish, alternating cheddar and cream cheese slices. To make a marinade, combine sugar, basil, salt, pepper, oil, vinegar, pimento, parsley, onion and garlic. Pour marinade over cheese, cover and refrigerate overnight. Garnish with fresh parsley sprigs.

Yield: 6 to 8 servings

Jezebel Sauce

1	(18 ounce) jar pineapple preserves		
1	(18 ounce) jar apple jelly	1	(1 ounce) can dry mustard
1	(2½ ounce) jar prepared horseradish	1	teaspoon white pepper

Combine preserves, jelly, horseradish, mustard and pepper. Blend thoroughly. Refrigerate at least 4 hours. Serve over cream cheese with crackers. Sauce will keep for several weeks in refrigerator.

Yield: 4 to 5 cups

Cheese Ring with Strawberry Preserves

1	pound cheddar cheese, shredded		Dash of black pepper
1	cup chopped nuts		Dash of cayenne pepper
1	cup mayonnaise	1	(18 ounce) jar strawberry preserves
1	small onion, grated or finely chopped		

Combine cheese, nuts, mayonnaise, onion, black pepper and cayenne pepper. Stir until well blended. Shape mixture into a circle or ball or press into a mold. Refrigerate at least 1 hour. If shaped into a circle, spoon preserves into the center. If shaped into a ball, spoon preserves over the top. Serve with crackers.

Yield: 8 to 12 servings

Fiery Tomato Cheese Spread

2   cups shredded sharp cheddar cheese
2   (3 ounce) packages cream cheese, softened
1   (7½ ounce) can tomatoes with green chiles

1½   teaspoons ground cumin
¾   teaspoon garlic powder

Combine cheeses, tomatoes and chiles, cumin and garlic powder in a bowl. Mix until smooth and chill. Serve with assorted crackers.

Yield: 6 servings

Black Olive Dip

2   (4¼ ounce) cans chopped black olives
1   purple onion, chopped
3   jalapeño peppers, chopped
1   large bell pepper, chopped

2   tablespoons oil
1   tomato, chopped
½   cup vinegar

Combine black olives, onion, peppers, oil, tomato and vinegar in a glass container. Marinate overnight. Serve with corn chips or tortilla chips.

Yield: 8 servings

Creamy Cheddar Cheese Ball

2	cups finely shredded cheddar cheese
1	(8 ounce) package cream cheese, softened
3	green onions, finely chopped
1	green bell pepper, finely chopped
1	(2 ounce) jar pimento, finely chopped
2	teaspoons Worcestershire sauce
2	cups crushed pecans

Combine cheeses in a mixing bowl until blended. Add onions, pepper, pimento and Worcestershire sauce and mix well. Form mixture into a ball. Roll ball in crushed pecans.

Yield: 6 to 12 servings

Curry Cheese Ball

1	(8 ounce) package cream cheese
1	cup shredded cheddar cheese
3	tablespoons sherry
1	tablespoon Worcestershire sauce
¾	teaspoon curry powder
½	teaspoon garlic powder
½	teaspoon white pepper
	Chopped peanuts, chopped green onion or shredded coconut

Combine cheeses, sherry, Worcestershire sauce, curry powder, garlic powder and white pepper. Form into a ball and chill. Top with choice of peanuts, onion or coconut.

Yield: 6 servings
This cheese ball freezes well.

Luau Cheese Ball

2 (8 ounce) packages cream cheese, softened	¼ cup chopped green bell pepper
1 (8 ounce) can crushed pineapple, drained well	2 tablespoons chopped onion
2 cups chopped pecans, divided	1 tablespoon seasoned salt

Combine cream cheese, pineapple, 1 cup pecans, bell pepper, onion and seasoned salt in a medium bowl. Mix well. Shape mixture into a ball. Roll ball in remaining pecans and transfer to a serving plate. Cover with plastic wrap and refrigerate overnight. Serve with your favorite crackers.

Yield: 8 to 12 servings

If desired, use 2 (8 ounce) tubs of pineapple cream cheese in place of the plain cream cheese and crushed pineapple.

Goat Cheese Dip

2 (3 ounce) logs goat cheese	¼ cup sliced chives
4 tablespoons butter	1 teaspoon salt
1 large clove garlic, pressed into paste	¼ cup chopped pistachio nuts, toasted and cooled

Combine cheese, butter, garlic, chives, salt and nuts in a mixing bowl. Serve with French bread slices or crackers.

Yield: 6 servings

South of the Border Layered Dip

1	(16 ounce) can refried beans		1	tomato, finely chopped, or to taste
1/2	(1¼ ounce) package taco seasoning mix		1	(4¼ ounce) can chopped black olives, or to taste
1	(6 ounce) container avocado dip		1	(4 ounce) can chopped green chiles, or to taste
1	(8 ounce) container sour cream		2	cups or more shredded Monterey Jack cheese
1	small onion, finely chopped, or to taste			

Spread beans on a medium to large serving platter. Sprinkle taco seasoning over beans. Spread avocado dip and then sour cream over beans. Sprinkle evenly with onion, tomato, olives and chiles. Top generously with cheese. Chill before serving. Can be prepared up to a day in advance. Serve with large corn chips or tortilla chips.

Yield: 12 servings

Cucumber Dip

2	large cucumbers, peeled and seeded		1	(8 ounce) package cream cheese, softened
1/2	small onion		1	tablespoon mayonnaise
				Seasoning salt to taste

Grate cucumber and onion and squeeze dry. Combine cream cheese, mayonnaise and seasoning salt in a bowl. Mix in cucumber and onion. Chill. Serve with vegetables or chips, or use as a filling for tea sandwiches.

Yield: 8 servings

Black Bean Salsa

2	(15 ounce) cans black beans, rinsed and drained	¼	cup chopped fresh cilantro
2	(17 ounce) cans shoepeg corn, drained	¼	cup lime juice
1	large tomato, seeded and chopped	2	tablespoons olive oil
1	large avocado, chopped	1	tablespoon red wine vinegar
1	purple onion, chopped		Salt and pepper to taste

Combine beans, corn, tomato, avocado, onion, cilantro, lime juice, oil, vinegar, salt and pepper in a large mixing bowl. Cover and chill. Serve with corn chips or tortilla chips.

Yield: 12 servings

El Presidente's Salsa

1	(4½ ounce) can chopped green chiles	1	large tomato, seeded and chopped
1	(4¼ ounce) can chopped black olives	⅔	cup Italian salad dressing
3	green onions, chopped	¼	cup fresh cilantro, chopped
2	cups shredded Monterey Jack cheese		

Combine chiles, olives, onion, cheese, tomato, dressing and cilantro in a medium bowl. Stir well. Serve with tortilla chips.

Yield: 3 to 4 cups

Sopapillas

1	(16 ounce) package large flour tortillas	½	cup cinnamon sugar
	Oil for frying		Honey to taste

Cut tortillas into strips or wedges. Heat oil in a skillet. Add tortilla pieces, a few at a time, and fry for a few seconds on each side. Remove tortilla pieces and drain on paper towels. While still warm, transfer pieces to a 9x13 inch pan and sprinkle with cinnamon sugar. Repeat until all tortilla pieces are fried, drained and sugared. Drizzle honey over sopapillas and serve.

Yield: about 5 dozen

Marshmallow Fruit Dip

1	(7 ounce) jar marshmallow creme	1	tablespoon orange juice
1	(8 ounce) package cream cheese, cubed and softened	1	teaspoon lemon zest, plus extra for garnish
1	teaspoon lemon juice	1	tablespoon orange zest, plus extra for garnish

Combine marshmallow creme, cream cheese, juices and zests in a mixing bowl. Beat with an electric mixer on medium speed until smooth. Chill before serving. Sprinkle with extra zest, if desired, to garnish. Serve with fresh strawberries or other seasonal fruits.

Yield: 12 servings

Benne Wafers

1	stick butter or margarine, softened	1	teaspoon vanilla
2	cups light brown sugar	1	cup self-rising flour
1	egg, beaten	1	cup benne seed (sesame seed)

Cream butter and sugar in a large bowl. Add egg and vanilla and mix well. Gradually add flour and benne seed, mixing well between additions. Divide dough into six equal parts. Roll each part into a 1 inch diameter log and wrap individually in foil. Freeze overnight or until ready to bake. When ready to bake, preheat oven to 325°. Slice frozen dough into thin circles and place on a foil-lined baking sheet. Bake at 325° for 8 to 10 minutes or until lightly browned. Cool thoroughly before removing from baking sheet.

Yield: 4 dozen

Parmesan Bacon Sticks

15	slices bacon, halved lengthwise	½-⅔	cup grated Parmesan cheese
1	(3 ounce) package Alessi thin breadsticks		

Preheat oven to 250°. Wrap bacon strips around breadsticks. Roll in cheese and place on baking sheets. Bake at 250° for 1 hour. Serve immediately.

Yield: 30 sticks

Spinach Balls

2	(10 ounce) packages frozen chopped spinach		½	cup Parmesan cheese, grated
1	(8 ounce) package dry stuffing mix		1	teaspoon garlic salt
1	medium onion, finely chopped			Pinch of thyme
4	eggs, beaten		½	tablespoon black pepper
1	stick butter, melted			

Preheat oven to 350°. Cook and drain spinach according to package directions. Combine cooked spinach with stuffing, onion, egg, butter, cheese, garlic salt, thyme and pepper. Shape mixture into 1 inch diameter balls. If desired, balls can be frozen at this point until ready to bake; remove frozen balls from freezer about 1 hour before baking. When ready to serve, place on lightly greased baked sheets and bake at 350° for 20 minutes or until lightly browned. Serve balls by themselves or with Honey Mustard Sauce (below).

Yield: 6 dozen

Honey Mustard Sauce

| 1 | cup mayonnaise | | ¼ | cup country-style Dijon mustard |
| ¼–⅓ | cup honey | | | Mrs. Dash seasoning |

Combine mayonnaise, honey and mustard. Season with Mrs. Dash. Mix well and chill. Vary ingredient amounts according to taste. Serve as a dip for Spinach Balls (above).

Yield: 1½ cups

Broccoli Squares

1	stick butter, melted	1	teaspoon salt
3	eggs	1	teaspoon baking powder
1	cup milk	1	cup flour
2	(10 ounce) packages frozen chopped broccoli, thawed and drained	2	cups shredded Monterey Jack cheese

Preheat oven to 350°. Pour butter into a 9x13 inch pan; set aside. Beat eggs in a large bowl. Add milk, broccoli, salt, baking powder and flour. Stir until well blended. Pour mixture over butter in pan. Sprinkle cheese on top. Bake at 350° for 40 to 45 minutes. Cool before cutting.

Yield: 8 servings

Michele's Bruschetta

1	loaf French baguette	1	(14½ ounce) can Italian diced tomatoes and herbs, drained
	Olive oil		Parmesan cheese to taste
1	(8 ounce) tub Alouette garlic and herb cheese spread		

Preheat broiler. Cut baguette into ¼ inch slices and place on a large baking sheet. Brush slices with olive oil. Spread with cheese spread. Spoon tomatoes on top and sprinkle with Parmesan cheese. Broil until edges are lightly browned. Serve immediately.

Yield: 12 servings

Bleu Cheese Balls

1	stick margarine	1	(7½ ounce) container refrigerated buttermilk biscuits
2	ounces bleu cheese		

Preheat oven to 350°. Melt margarine and bleu cheese in a saucepan. Quarter each biscuit and roll dough pieces into balls. Place balls in a 9 inch round pan. Pour margarine mixture over balls. Bake at 350° for 10 to 15 minutes.

Yield: 8 servings

Blue Cheese Crisps

1	stick butter or margarine, softened	1	(4 ounce) package crumbled blue cheese, softened
½	cup chopped pecans	1	loaf French baguette, sliced

Preheat oven to 350°. Cream butter and cheese together. Stir in pecans. Set aside. Place bread slices in a single layer on baking sheets. Bake at 350° for 3 to 5 minutes. Turn slices and spread evenly with cheese mixture. Bake 5 minutes longer. Serve immediately.

Yield: 32 appetizers

Cheese Goodies

1 cup shredded cheddar cheese
½-¾ cup chopped green onion
1 (4¼ ounce) can chopped black olives

4 tablespoons mayonnaise
1 loaf sourdough French bread, sliced
Parmesan cheese

Preheat broiler. Combine cheddar cheese, onion, olives and mayonnaise. Spread mixture over bread slices. Sprinkle Parmesan cheese on top. Broil until bubbly.

Yield: 6 servings

Cocktail Cheese Wafers

1 stick butter, softened
1 cup shredded sharp cheddar cheese
1 teaspoon salt

½ teaspoon cayenne pepper
1 cup flour
48 pecan halves

Preheat oven to 350°. Cream butter in a large bowl. Blend in cheese. Stir in salt, pepper and flour. Mix thoroughly. Roll dough into small balls. Press one pecan half onto each ball to flatten. Place balls on an ungreased baking sheet. Bake at 350° for 15 minutes.

Yield: about 4 dozen, 12 servings

Sausage Cheese Balls

3	cups baking mix	1	pound bulk sausage
4	cups shredded cheddar cheese	½	cup Parmesan cheese

Preheat oven to 350°. Combine baking mix, sausage and cheeses. Shape mixture into 1 inch balls and place in a greased jelly-roll pan. Bake at 350° for 20 to 25 minutes or until browned. Remove immediately from pan. Serve warm with barbecue or chili sauce for dipping.

Yield: 6½ dozen

Georgia Bull "Dawg Chow"

6	cups Rice Chex cereal	47	caramels
2	cups pecan halves	¼	cup water

Preheat oven to 250°. Combine cereal and pecans in a large bowl; set aside. Place caramels and water in a microwavable bowl and microwave on high for 2 minutes; check every 30 seconds and stir occasionally. Pour melted caramel over cereal mixture. Stir until evenly coated. Spread mixture on ungreased baking sheets. Bake at 250° for 20 minutes, turning mixture once while baking. Remove mixture from baking sheets and store in an airtight container. Soak baking sheets in warm water to loosen excess caramel.

Yield: 2 to 3 dozen servings

White Chocolate Party Mix

1   (10 ounce) package mini pretzels
5   cups Cheerios cereal
5   cups Corn Chex cereal
2   cups salted peanuts

1   (1 pound) package plain M&M's
2   (12 ounce) packages vanilla chips
3   tablespoons vegetable oil

Combine pretzels, Cheerios, Corn Chex, peanuts and M&M's in a large bowl; set aside. In a microwavable bowl, microwave vanilla chips and oil at medium-high for 2 minutes, stirring once. Microwave on high for 10 seconds and stir until smooth. Pour over cereal mixture and mix well until evenly coated. Spread mixture onto 3 wax paper-lined baking sheets. Cool and break apart. Store in an airtight container.

Yield: 5 quarts

Alabama Cheese Nips

1   (1 ounce) package dry Ranch dressing mix
½   cup vegetable oil
2   teaspoons dill weed

Dash of garlic powder
Dash of cayenne pepper
1   (1 pound) box square cheese crackers

Combine dressing mix, oil, dill, garlic powder and cayenne pepper. Pour mixture over crackers and stir well until coated.

Yield: 8 to 12 servings

Nuts and Bolts

2	**sticks butter, melted**
1	**teaspoon celery salt**
1	**teaspoon onion salt**
½	**teaspoon garlic powder**
2	**tablespoons Worcestershire sauce**
3	**cups Cheerios cereal**

4	**cups Rice Chex cereal**
3	**cups Wheat Chex cereal**
2	**cups mini pretzels**
1	**cup cheese crackers**
1	**cup snack-size garlic chips**
2	**cups mixed nuts**

Preheat oven to 250°. Combine butter, celery salt, onion salt, garlic powder and Worcestershire sauce. In a separate bowl, combine cereals, pretzels, crackers, garlic chips and nuts. Pour seasoning mixture over cereal mixture and stir gently until evenly coated. Transfer to a large roasting pan. Bake at 250° for 2 hours, stirring every 15 minutes. Spread mixture onto paper towels to cool. Store in an airtight container.

Yield: 16 cups

Southern Stuffed Mushrooms

¾ pound bacon, cooked crisp and crumbled
1 (8 ounce) package cream cheese, softened
1 small bunch green onions, finely chopped

1 (16 ounce) container fresh mushrooms, washed, stems discarded

Preheat oven to 350°. Combine bacon, cream cheese and onions. Mix thoroughly and stuff into mushroom caps to the rim. Place on a baking sheet, stuffing-side up. Bake at 350° for 15 minutes. Serve immediately.

Yield: 6 servings

Bleu Cheese Mushrooms

1 teaspoon chopped onion
1 stick butter
1 ounce bleu cheese
½ cup dry stuffing mix
   Dash of garlic powder

Dash of oregano
Dash of parsley
Dash of black pepper
1 pound fresh mushrooms, stems discarded

Preheat oven to 400°. Sauté onion in butter in a saucepan. In a mixing bowl, beat cheese with an electric mixer until smooth. Add sautéed onion, stuffing, garlic powder, oregano, parsley and black pepper to bowl. Mix well. Stuff mixture into mushroom caps. Bake at 400° for 10 to 15 minutes.

Yield: 8 servings

Crab Stuffed Mushrooms

12	large mushroom caps	2	tablespoons chopped onion
2	tablespoons vegetable oil	1	teaspoon lemon juice
1	(6 ounce) package crabmeat	½	cup cubed soft bread, divided
2	tablespoons mayonnaise	2	tablespoons butter, melted
1	egg, lightly beaten		

Preheat oven to 375°. Wash and pat dry mushroom caps. Brush with oil and placed in a greased baking dish. In a mixing bowl, combine crabmeat, mayonnaise, egg, onion, lemon juice, and ¼ cup bread. Mix well and stuff into mushroom caps. Combine butter and remaining ¼ cup bread. Divide bread among tops of stuffed mushrooms. Bake at 375° for about 15 minutes.

Yield: 6 servings

For variety, add ½ cup shredded Swiss cheese to the crab mixture.

Scrumptious Hot Crab Dip

2	tablespoons butter
2	tablespoons all-purpose flour
1½	cups milk or half-and-half
1	cup shredded sharp cheddar cheese

	Dash of black pepper
¼	cup bread crumbs
1	pound lump crabmeat

Preheat oven to 350°. Combine butter, flour, milk, cheese, pepper, crumbs and crabmeat. Bake at 350° for 10 to 20 minutes.

Yield: 6 servings

Crab Muffins

1	stick margarine, softened
1	(5 ounce) jar Old English cheese, room temperature
6	ounces lump crabmeat
2	teaspoons minced green onion

	Dash of seasoned salt
	Dash of Worcestershire sauce
10	English muffins, halved

Beat margarine and cheese together in a large mixing bowl. Stir in crabmeat, onion, seasoned salt and Worcestershire sauce. Spread mixture over muffin halves. Place halves on a baking sheet and refrigerate 1 hour. Preheat oven to 400°. Cut each half into 6 wedges. Bake at 400° for 15 minutes, then broil for 1 to 2 minutes or until golden brown.

Yield: 20 servings

Hot Curried Crab Dip

¼	pound king crabmeat
1	(8 ounce) package cream cheese with chives, softened
1	tablespoon mayonnaise
½	onion, grated
½	teaspoon curry powder
1	teaspoon horseradish
2	tablespoons milk
1	tablespoon Worcestershire sauce
	Salt and pepper to taste

Combine crabmeat, cream cheese, mayonnaise, onion, curry powder, horseradish, milk, Worcestershire sauce, salt and pepper in a large mixing bowl. Transfer to the top of a double boiler and heat until hot. Serve in a chafing dish with assorted chips.

Yield: 8 servings

Mother Duvall's Crab Cakes

1   **pound crabmeat**
4   **heaping tablespoons mayonnaise**
½   **teaspoon Worcestershire sauce**
½   **teaspoon cayenne pepper**
¼   **teaspoon salt**

½   **small onion, grated**
½   **tablespoon dry mustard**
18   **round butter crackers, crumbled**
      Butter for sautéing

Combine crabmeat, mayonnaise, Worcestershire sauce, cayenne pepper, salt, onion and mustard. Stir in cracker crumbs just prior to cooking to prevent them from getting too moist. Shape mixture into hamburger-size patties to serve as an entrée or small patties for hors d'oeuvres. Sauté in butter in a skillet over medium to high heat for 10 minutes on each side. Crab cake should be crispy on the outside but moist and juicy inside. Serve with tartar sauce.

Yield: 6 entrée servings or 15 to 18 hors d'oeuvres.

Jumbo crab is best used for the large patties but not for the smaller ones. Back-fin or lump crabmeat is good for either size.

Make homemade tartar sauce by combining desired amounts of mayonnaise, grated onion and lemon juice.

Cream Cheese and Crab Spread

2	tablespoons minced onion	½	(12 ounce) bottle chili sauce
1	(8 ounce) plus 1 (3 ounce) package cream cheese	1	(6 ounce) can crabmeat
2	tablespoons Worcestershire sauce	⅓	cup chopped green onion
½	teaspoon seasoned salt		

Soak onion in water until softened; drain. Combine onion, cream cheese, Worcestershire sauce and seasoned salt in a medium mixing bowl. Beat with an electric mixer until well blended. Spread mixture on a plate about ¼ inch thick. Spread chili sauce evenly over mixture. Sprinkle crabmeat on top. Garnish with green onion and serve with crackers.

Yield: 8 servings

Hot Shrimp Dip

1	(8 ounce) package cream cheese, cubed and softened	1½	teaspoons seasoning blend
1	(4 ounce) can cocktail shrimp, rinsed, drained and chopped	½	teaspoon milk
¼	cup minced onion		Slivered almonds, optional
1½	teaspoons horseradish		

Combine cream cheese, shrimp, onion, horseradish, seasoning blend and milk until well mixed. Place in a 2 cup oven-proof baking dish and top with almonds. Refrigerate at least 8 hours or overnight. When ready to serve, preheat oven to 350°. Bake at 350° for 15 minutes or until heated through. Serve hot with crackers.

Yield: 6 servings

"A Day at the Beach" Hot Seafood Dip

1   (6 ounce) can cocktail shrimp, finely chopped
8   ounces imitation crabmeat, finely chopped
2   (8 ounce) packages cream cheese, cubed and softened
1   cup shredded cheddar cheese
½   (4 ounce) can chopped green chiles

¼   cup mayonnaise
    Juice of ½ lemon
1   teaspoon dry mustard
    Garlic powder to taste
    Paprika or cayenne pepper

Preheat oven to 350°. Combine shrimp, crabmeat, cheeses, chiles, mayonnaise, lemon juice, mustard and garlic powder in a large bowl. Blend well with an electric mixer. Pour mixture into a large casserole dish. Sprinkle with paprika for color and taste. Bake at 350° for 30 minutes. Serve with large corn chips or assorted crackers.

Yield: 15 to 20 servings

Shrimply Devine

1   (3 ounce) package cream cheese, softened
1   cup sour cream
2   teaspoons lemon juice

1   (1 ounce) package dry Italian salad dressing mix
½   cup drained and chopped canned shrimp

Combine cream cheese, sour cream, lemon juice, dressing mix and shrimp in a blender. Process until smooth. Chill. Serve with fresh vegetables or crackers.

Yield: 6 servings

Smoked Salmon Mousse

13-14 ounces smoked salmon, divided

½ cup plain yogurt

¼-½ teaspoon cayenne pepper

½ teaspoon paprika

2 tablespoons extra virgin olive oil

Zest of 1 lemon

2 tablespoons lemon juice

Chop half the salmon and put in a food processor. Add yogurt, cayenne pepper, paprika, olive oil, lemon zest and juice. Process ingredients until mixture is a thin purée. Coarsely chop remaining half of salmon and stir into purée. Mix well and chill. Serve with assorted crackers.

Yield: 8 servings

Ad-In, Ad-Out: Breads, Soups, Salads & Dressings

Michael, grade 3 • Hickory Flat Elementary

Melissa's Blue Ribbon Orange Bread

¾ cup granulated sugar
1 cup chopped pecans or walnuts
1 tablespoon grated orange rind
2 (10 ounce) cans buttermilk biscuits

1 (8 ounce) tub cream cheese (not whipped), softened
1 stick butter, melted
1 cup sifted powder sugar
2 tablespoons orange juice

Preheat oven to 350°. Combine granulated sugar, pecans and rind; set aside. Separate biscuits and spread each with cream cheese, then dip in butter and roll in sugar mixture. Stand biscuits upright on edge in a greased Bundt pan, spacing evenly. Drizzle any remaining butter and sugar mixture over biscuits. Bake at 350° for 45 minutes or until golden brown. While baking, combine powdered sugar and juice to make a glaze. When bread is done baking, immediately invert bread onto a serving platter and drizzle with glaze.

Yield: 12 servings

Sour Cream Muffins

1 cup self-rising flour
1 stick butter, melted

1 cup sour cream

Preheat oven to 350°. Stir together flour, butter and sour cream in a medium bowl. Mix well. Divide batter among greased mini muffin tins. Bake at 350° for 20 minutes or until edges brown.

Yield: 12 servings

Strawberry Bread

3	**cups all-purpose flour**		**4**	**eggs, beaten**
2	**cups sugar**		**1¼**	**cups oil**
1	**tablespoon cinnamon**		**1**	**cup chopped pecans**
1	**teaspoon baking soda**		**1**	**(10 ounce) package frozen strawberries, thawed**
1	**teaspoon salt**			

Preheat oven to 325°. Combine flour and sugar in a mixing bowl. Add cinnamon, baking soda and salt. Mix well. Stir in eggs and oil. Fold in pecans and strawberries. Pour batter into 2 greased and floured loaf pans. Bake at 325° for 1 hour.

Yield: 2 loaves

Muffins

3	**tablespoons sugar**		**1**	**(18 ounce) package blueberry muffin mix**
½	**teaspoon cinnamon**		**2**	**tablespoons butter or margarine, melted**

Combine sugar and cinnamon; set aside. Prepare muffins as directed on package. Cool muffins in pan for about 5 minutes. Remove muffins from pan. Dip top of hot muffins in melted butter, then dip in cinnamon sugar mixture.

Yield: 12 muffins

Apricot Pound Loaf

2   (3 ounce) packages orange jello
1   (12 ounce) can apricot nectar, heated
2   (16 ounce) boxes dry pound cake mix
1¼ cups vegetable oil

6   eggs
2   cups powdered sugar
    Juice of 2 lemons

Preheat oven to 325°. Dissolve jello in heated nectar; cool. Stir in cake mix. Add oil. Beat in eggs one at a time. Divide batter between 3 greased and floured loaf pans. Bake at 325° for 1 hour. Combine sugar and lemon juice to make a glaze. Drizzle glaze over hot loaves.

Yield: 3 loaves

Loaves can be frozen. Freezing seems to enhance flavor.

Beer Bread

3	cups self-rising flour	1	(12 ounce) can beer, room temperature
3	tablespoons sugar		

Preheat oven to 350°. Combine flour, sugar and beer in a large bowl. Pour batter into 2 greased loaf pans. Bake at 350° for 1 hour.

Yield: 2 loaves

Lemon Blueberry Poppy Seed Bread

1	(23½ ounce) package bakery-style blueberry muffin mix with	¾	cup water
	crumb topping	1	tablespoon grated lemon rind
2	tablespoons poppy seeds	½	cup powdered sugar
1	egg	1	tablespoon lemon juice

Preheat oven to 350°. Rinse blueberries from mix with cold water; drain. Empty dry muffin mix into a medium mixing bowl. Stir in poppy seeds. Stir in egg and water. Fold in blueberries and rind. Pour batter into a greased and floured 4x8 inch loaf pan. Sprinkle crumb topping from mix over batter. Bake at 350° for 55 to 60 minutes. Cool in pan 10 minutes. Remove from pan and cool completely. Combine sugar and juice to make a glaze. Drizzle glaze over cooled bread.

Yield: 1 loaf

Blueberry Coffeecake

CAKE

¾ cup sugar
4 tablespoons butter (not margarine), softened
1 egg

TOPPING

½ cup sugar
⅓ cup all-purpose flour

2 cups all-purpose flour
2 teaspoons baking powder
½ teaspoon salt
½ cup milk
2 cups blueberries, washed and stemmed

½ teaspoon cinnamon
4 tablespoons butter (not margarine), softened

Preheat oven to 350°. To prepare cake, cream together sugar, butter and egg. In a separate bowl, sift together flour, baking powder and salt. Add dry ingredients and milk to creamed mixture alternately. Carefully fold in blueberries. Pour batter into a greased 9 inch square baking pan.

To make topping, combine sugar, flour, cinnamon and butter. Sprinkle mixture over cake batter. Bake cake at 350° for 40 to 45 minutes.

Yield: 8 servings

Banana Bread ✳

2	**sticks margarine**
2	**cups sugar**
2	**teaspoons vanilla**
2	**teaspoons lemon juice**
4	**eggs**
1	**teaspoon salt**

3½	**cups all-purpose flour**
2	**teaspoons baking soda**
2	**teaspoons baking powder**
6	**bananas, mashed**
1	**cup sour cream**
½	**cup chopped nuts, optional**

Preheat oven to 325°. Cream margarine and sugar. Add vanilla, juice and eggs. In a separate bowl, sift together salt, flour, baking soda and baking powder. Stir dry ingredients into margarine mixture. Mix in bananas, sour cream and nuts. Pour batter into 2 greased 9x5 inch loaf pans. Bake at 325° for 90 minutes or until bread springs back when touched.

Yield: 2 loaves

Pineapple-Zucchini Bread

3	cups flour	3	eggs, beaten
½	teaspoon salt	1	cup vegetable oil
1	teaspoon baking soda	2	cups coarsely shredded zucchini (about ¾ pound)
2	cups sugar	1	(20 ounce) can crushed pineapple, drained
1	teaspoon cinnamon	2	teaspoons vanilla
1	cup chopped walnuts or pecans		

Preheat oven to 350°. Combine flour, salt, baking soda, sugar and cinnamon in a large mixing bowl. Stir in walnuts. In a separate bowl, combine egg, oil, zucchini, pineapple and vanilla. Add zucchini mixture to dry ingredients, stirring just until dry ingredients are moistened. Spoon batter into 2 greased and floured 9x5 inch loaf pans. Bake at 350° for 70 minutes or until a toothpick inserted in the center comes out clean. Cool in pans 10 minutes. Remove from pans and cool on a wire rack.

Yield: 2 loaves

Aunt Minnie's Many Mini Blintzes

½	cup granulated sugar		1	tablespoon cinnamon
2	egg yolks		1	(2 pound) loaf thin sliced fresh white bread, crusts removed
2	(8 ounce) packages cream cheese, softened		2	sticks butter, melted
½	cup brown sugar			

Preheat oven to 350°. Cream granulated sugar, yolks and cream cheese together; set aside. In a separate bowl, combine brown sugar and cinnamon; set aside. Roll each slice of bread very thin. Spread slices with cream cheese mixture and roll into logs. Dip in melted butter, then roll in cinnamon sugar mixture. Cinnamon sugar mixture may need to be replenished depending on how coating is applied. Cut rolls in half and place on a baking sheet. Bake at 350° for 20 minutes.

Yield: 12 servings

These are great to make ahead of time. Place sugar-coated rolls on baking sheet and freeze for 20 minutes or until firm. Transfer to a plastic bag until ready to bake. Thaw on a baking sheet before baking as directed above.

Broccoli Cornbread

1	(10 ounce) package frozen chopped broccoli	1	(6 ounce) box Jiffy cornbread mix
¾	cup cottage cheese	1	stick butter or margarine, melted
4	eggs, beaten	⅓	cup chopped onion
1	teaspoon salt		

Preheat oven to 400°. Cook broccoli in boiling water until no longer frozen. Drain and set aside. Combine cottage cheese, egg, salt, cornbread mix, butter and onion in a large bowl. Stir in broccoli until well blended. Pour batter into a 9x13 inch pan. Bake at 400° for 25 minutes.

Yield: 16 servings

This cornbread makes a wonderful appetizer if cut into smaller portions.

Parmesan-Wine Bread

2	cups biscuit mix	**4**	tablespoons butter, melted
1	tablespoon sugar	**¼**	cup dry white wine
½	teaspoon dried oregano	**1**	egg, lightly beaten
½	cup Parmesan cheese, divided	**½**	cup milk

Preheat oven to 400°. Combine biscuit mix, sugar and oregano in a mixing bowl. Stir in ¼ cup cheese, butter, wine, egg and milk. Spoon batter into a greased 8 inch pie plate or round cake pan. Sprinkle with remaining ¼ cup cheese. Bake at 400° for 20 to 25 minutes. Serve warm.

Yield: 1 loaf

Pull-Apart Parmesan Rolls

1	pound frozen bread dough, thawed	**6**	tablespoons Parmesan cheese
1	teaspoon garlic powder	**1**	stick margarine, melted

Cut dough into 16 pieces. Shape into balls and place on a floured surface. Cover and let rise for 10 minutes. In a small bowl, stir together cheese, garlic powder and butter. Using a spoon, roll each ball in cheese mixture. Arrange balls loosely in a 9 inch round baking dish. Cover and let rise in a warm place until doubled. When ready to bake, preheat oven to 375°. Bake at 375° for 10 to 15 minutes. Serve warm.

Yield: 8 servings

French Bread Spread

2 sticks margarine, softened	**½** teaspoon paprika
1 cup shredded sharp cheddar cheese	**¼** teaspoon garlic powder
¼ cup Parmesan cheese	**2** loaves French bread, sliced lengthwise
1 teaspoon Worcestershire sauce	

Combine margarine, cheeses, Worcestershire sauce, paprika and garlic powder. Whip until blended. Spread on cut side of bread. Broil bread until bubbly. Serve hot.

Yield: 12 servings

Creole Black-Eyed Pea Soup

1	(16 ounce) package dried black-eyed peas	1	teaspoon cayenne pepper	
8	ounces ham hock	1	teaspoon black pepper	
3	medium onions, chopped	3	dashes Tabasco sauce	
1	bunch green onions, chopped	1	tablespoon Worcestershire sauce	
1	cup chopped fresh parsley	3	(8 ounce) cans peeled tomatoes, chopped	
1	green bell pepper, chopped	¼	teaspoon oregano	
2	cloves garlic, minced	¼	teaspoon thyme	
1½	teaspoons salt	1	pound smoked sausage, sliced and browned	

Soak peas for 1 hour in cold water; drain. Combine peas and ham hock in a large pot. Add water to cover and cook until peas are almost done. Add onions, parsley, bell pepper, garlic, salt, cayenne pepper, black pepper, Tabasco sauce, Worcestershire sauce, tomatoes, oregano, thyme and sausage. Simmer several hours. Serve over hot rice.

Yield: 8 to 12 servings

This recipe is good made 1 to 2 days in advance. It can also be frozen for longer periods until ready to serve.

Bayou Étouffée

1	cup finely chopped onion		1	pound medium to large crawfish or shrimp tails, peeled
2	tablespoons finely chopped shallot		1	tablespoon cornstarch
½	cup finely chopped celery		1	teaspoon Accent
½	cup chopped bell pepper		¼	teaspoon cayenne pepper or to taste
2	tablespoons finely chopped garlic		2	tablespoons Worcestershire sauce
4	tablespoons butter		½	cup canned condensed cream of mushroom soup

Sauté onion, shallot, celery, bell pepper and garlic in butter until soft. Add crawfish and simmer over low heat for 10 minutes, stirring frequently. In a bowl, combine cornstarch with enough water to make a thin paste. Add Accent, cayenne pepper, Worcestershire sauce and soup. Stir soup mixture into crawfish mixture. Bring to a boil. Reduce heat and simmer 20 minutes to blend flavors. Serve over rice.

Yield: 6 servings

Italian Vegetable Soup

1	pound ground beef
1	cup diced onion
2	cloves garlic, minced
1	(15 ounce) can red kidney beans
5	teaspoons dry beef bouillon
1	tablespoon dried parsley
1	cup sliced carrot
1	cup sliced celery
1	(16 ounce) can whole tomatoes

1	(15 ounce) can tomato sauce
2	cups water
½	teaspoon basil
1	teaspoon salt
½	teaspoon black pepper
2	cups shredded cabbage
½	cup dry small elbow macaroni
	Parmesan cheese

Brown ground beef in a large pot; drain. Add onion, garlic, beans, bouillon, parsley, carrot, celery, tomatoes, tomato sauce, water, salt, basil and pepper. Bring to a boil. Reduce heat to a simmer, cover and cook 20 minutes. Add cabbage and macaroni. Bring to a boil. Reduce heat to a simmer and cook until vegetables are tender. Add extra water if a thinner soup is desired. Sprinkle with Parmesan cheese before serving.

Yield: 6 servings

White Chili

2	medium onions, chopped	1	(10 ounce) can Mexican corn, drained
½	tablespoon olive oil	2	(14½ ounce) cans great Northern beans, drained
2	tablespoons minced garlic	2	cups chopped cooked chicken
2	teaspoons ground cumin	1	(14½ ounce) can stewed Mexican tomatoes
1½	teaspoons oregano	2	teaspoons dried cilantro leaves
1	teaspoon white pepper	1	(8 ounce) container sour cream
2	(4 ounce) cans chopped green chiles	2	cups shredded cheese
3	(14½ ounce) cans chicken broth, plus 1 can water		Large corn chips

Cook onion in oil in a 6 quart pot until tender. Remove from heat and mix in garlic, cumin, oregano and white pepper. Stir in chiles, broth, water and corn. Mix in beans, chicken, tomatoes and cilantro. Stir to mix well. Cover and cook over medium to low heat for 2 hours, stirring occasionally. Top individual servings with sour cream, cheese and corn chips.

Yield: 8 servings

Chili Kahlúa

¼	cup vegetable oil		1	teaspoon oregano, crushed
2	onions, chopped		1	teaspoon cumin, crushed
2	cloves garlic, minced		3	tablespoons chili powder
2	pounds ground beef		2	teaspoons salt
½	bell pepper, cut into chunks		1	scant teaspoon cayenne pepper
1	(28 ounce) can crushed tomatoes		½	cup Kahlúa
1	tablespoon tomato paste or to taste		1	(27 ounce) can red kidney beans, partially drained
¼	cup chopped parsley			Shredded cheddar cheese and chopped onion for garnish
1	teaspoon marjoram, crushed			

Heat oil in a 4 quart pot. Add onion and garlic and sauté until soft. Add beef and crumble and stir until browned. Add bell pepper, tomatoes, tomato paste, parsley, marjoram, oregano, cumin, chili powder, salt and cayenne pepper. Mix thoroughly. Add Kahlúa and increase heat to a simmer. Add beans and simmer, partially covered, for 45 minutes. Garnish individual servings with cheese and chopped onion.

Yield: 2½ quarts, 6 servings

When done cooking, spoon mixture into corn or flour tortillas and roll into enchiladas. Place in a baking dish, seam-side down, and cover with your favorite enchilada sauce flavored with 2 tablespoons Kahlúa. Sprinkle cheddar cheese on top and broil 3 minutes or until cheese melts.

Savory Seafood Chowder

1	(7½ ounce) can crabmeat		⅛	teaspoon black pepper
1	(4½) ounce can shrimp		½	teaspoon thyme
1	(8 ounce) can minced clams		1	(16 ounce) can cream-style corn
4	strips bacon, diced		2	cups milk
1	clove garlic, minced		2	cups half-and-half or cream
2	cups diced potatoes		½	cup chopped green onion
1	cup chicken broth		2	tablespoons minced parsley
1½	teaspoons salt			

Drain seafood, reserving liquid. Slice crab. In a large saucepan, sauté bacon and garlic until bacon is crisp. Add potatoes, reserved seafood liquid, broth, salt, pepper and thyme. Cover and simmer 15 to 20 minutes or until potatoes are tender. Add seafood, corn, milk, half-and-half, onion and parsley. Heat slowly to a simmer but do not boil.

Yield: 8 servings

Shrimp Confetti Soup

1/4	cup vegetable oil	2	cups cream-style corn
1	cup chopped yellow onion	1	cup whole kernel corn
1/2	cup chopped green bell pepper	1/2	cup canned, chopped and drained tomatoes with green chiles
1/2	cup chopped red bell pepper	1	tablespoon chopped fresh thyme
1/4	cup chopped celery	1/2	tablespoon chopped fresh sage
2	tablespoons chopped garlic	2	tablespoon chopped fresh parsley
1	pound medium shrimp, peeled	1/2	cup diagonally-cut green onion
2	cups chicken broth	1	cup shredded mozzarella cheese
1	quart heavy cream		

Heat oil in a large heavy pot. Add yellow onion, bell peppers, celery, garlic and shrimp. Sauté over high heat for 5 minutes. Add broth, cream, cream-style and whole kernel corn, tomatoes with chiles, thyme, sage and parsley. Reduce heat to medium and cook 25 minutes, stirring occasionally. Garnish individual servings with green onion and cheese.

Yield: 8 servings

This soup can be prepared a day in advance.

The Ultimate Greek Salad

2   heads Iceberg lettuce
3   cups Greek Potato Salad (see page 74)
2   tomatoes, seeded and chopped
1   cucumber, peeled and chopped into ½ inch pieces
     Feta cheese
½   green bell pepper, cut into 12 slices
12   red beet slices
12   shrimp, cooked and peeled
     Anchovy fillets

     Greek olives
     Hot peppers
     Sliced radishes
     Whole green onions
½   cup white vinegar
¼   cup olive oil
¼   cup vegetable oil
     Oregano to taste

Line an extra large serving bowl with outer lettuce leaves. Chop remaining lettuce into bite-size pieces. Place potato salad in a mound in the center of the bowl. Cover potato salad with chopped lettuce. Sprinkle with tomato and cucumber. Crumble a generous amount of Feta cheese on top and arrange bell pepper slices around the bowl. Place beet slices between bell pepper slices and top each beet with a shrimp. Arrange anchovy fillets, olives, hot peppers, radishes and green onions on top according to preference. Refrigerate until ready to serve. Pour vinegar over entire salad. Blend oils and pour over salad. Sprinkle with oregano to taste. Toss to allow vinegar and oils to coat salad. Serve immediately.

Yield: 8 to 12 servings

This salad is easiest when Greek Potato Salad is made the day before.

Greek Potato Salad

6	**boiling potatoes**		**¼**	**cup finely chopped parsley**
1	**medium white onion, chopped**			**Salt to taste**
½	**cup thinly sliced green onion**		**¾**	**cup mayonnaise**
½	**green bell pepper, chopped**			

Boil unpeeled potatoes for 20 to 30 minutes or until tender but not soft. Drain and cool. Peel potatoes and cube; place in a bowl. Add onions, bell pepper, parsley and salt. Fold in mayonnaise, using more if needed to hold salad together. Mix until well blended. Chill before serving.

Yield: 3 to 4 cups

Old-Fashioned Potato Salad

3	pounds redskin potatoes		½	teaspoon black pepper
¼	cup wine vinegar		4	hard-cooked eggs, chopped
1	cup chopped celery		¼	cup sugar
½	cup chopped green onion		1	cup mayonnaise-type salad dressing
1	teaspoon salt			

Boil whole potatoes until tender. Drain and place in a mixing bowl. Pour vinegar over hot potatoes. When potatoes cool, chop and return to bowl; reserving any remaining vinegar on the side. Add celery and onion to bowl. In a separate bowl, mix together salt, pepper, egg, sugar, salad dressing and reserved vinegar. Pour over potato mixture and mix gently. Refrigerate until chilled.

Yield: 12 servings

Creole Potato Salad

3	pounds red potatoes, cubed
1/2	cup mayonnaise
1/2	cup Creole mustard
1	tablespoon red wine vinegar
1	teaspoon salt
1	teaspoon prepared horseradish

1/2	teaspoon dried thyme
1/4	teaspoon garlic powder
1/4	teaspoon cayenne pepper
6	hard-cooked eggs, chopped
1	medium-size sweet onion, diced

Cover potatoes in a saucepan with salted water and bring to a boil. Cook 12 minutes or until tender; drain and cool slightly. In a large bowl, combine mayonnaise, mustard, vinegar, salt, horseradish, thyme, garlic powder and cayenne pepper. Gently fold in the potatoes, egg and onion. Serve chilled.

Yield: 8 servings

Summertime Picnic Salad

6 tablespoons sugar
¼ cup oil
6 tablespoons white vinegar
   Pinch of favorite herbs, such as basil, oregano and black
      pepper
1 (16 ounce) can English peas, drained

1 (16 ounce) can French-style green beans, drained
1 (12 ounce) can shoepeg corn, drained
1 cup finely chopped celery
1 cup finely chopped onion
1 (2 ounce) chopped pimento, drained

Combine sugar, oil, vinegar and herbs in a saucepan. Cook and stir over medium heat until sugar dissolves. Remove marinade from heat and cool. In a medium bowl, combine peas, beans, corn, celery, onion and pimento. Pour cooled marinade over vegetables. Cover and refrigerate at least 8 hours or overnight. Stir occasionally to coat vegetables.

Yield: 12 servings

Carolina Slaw

1	large head cabbage, grated, or 1 (16 ounce) package broccoli/cabbage slaw mix		1	teaspoon dry mustard
¾	cup plus 2 teaspoons sugar, divided		1	teaspoon celery salt
1	cup distilled vinegar		1	tablespoon salt
			¼	cup vegetable oil

Place grated cabbage in a large bowl. Pour ¾ cup sugar over cabbage. In a small saucepan, bring vinegar, 2 teaspoons sugar, mustard, celery salt, salt and oil to a boil. Pour mixture over cabbage. Refrigerate overnight.

Yield: 6 to 8 servings

Slaw keeps up to 10 days in refrigerator. Oil may be omitted to reduce fat.

Oriental Cole Slaw

1   (3 ounce) package ramen noodles, any flavor
1   (16 ounce) package coleslaw mix
1   (6 ounce) package sunflower seed kernels
2   (2 ounce) packages slivered almonds

1   bunch green onions, chopped
¾   cup oil
⅓   cup vinegar
½   cup sugar

Crumble noodles, reserving flavor packet. Combine coleslaw mix, sunflower seeds, almonds and onion in a large bowl. Heat oil, vinegar and sugar until sugar dissolves. Add flavor packet to heated dressing. Pour dressing over coleslaw mixture and transfer to an airtight container. Refrigerate at least 30 minutes or overnight. When ready to serve, toss in crumbled noodles.

Yield: 8 to 12 servings

Great recipe for picnics or large groups. Turn recipe into a main dish by adding cooked shrimp, ham, chicken or turkey.

Marinated Asparagus

1½-2	**pounds fresh asparagus**	⅓	**cup red wine vinegar**
1	**medium green bell pepper, chopped**	⅓	**cup sugar**
4-5	**green onions, chopped**	½	**clove garlic, finely chopped**
1	**stalk celery, finely chopped**	¼	**teaspoon paprika**
¾	**cup vegetable oil**		**Pimento strips**

Steam asparagus 5 minutes; drain and place in a 9x13 inch baking dish. Combine bell pepper, onion, celery, oil, vinegar, sugar, garlic and paprika and pour mixture over asparagus. Cover and chill 4 hours or overnight. When ready to serve, drain marinade and garnish with pimento strips. Serve as is or on a bed of lettuce.

Yield: 6 to 8 servings

Tennis Time Broccoli Salad

1   bunch fresh broccoli
1   cup shredded mozzarella or cheddar cheese, or combination
½   cup chopped red onion
1   cup mayonnaise

½   cup sugar
¼   cup red wine vinegar
6   slices bacon, cooked and crumbled

Cut away and discard broccoli stalks or save for another use. Cut broccoli florets into bite-size pieces. In a large bowl, combine florets, cheese and onion. Toss well. In a separate bowl, combine mayonnaise, sugar and vinegar for a dressing. Just before serving, add dressing and bacon to broccoli mixture and toss.

Yield: 6 servings

For a slightly different variation, add ½ cup golden raisins and/or 1 cup cashew pieces sautéed in butter.

Cauliflower Salad

1	head lettuce, shredded		1/4	cup sugar
1	head cauliflower, chopped		1/2	cup grated Parmesan cheese
1	medium onion, chopped		8	ounces bacon, cooked and crumbled
1 1/2	cups mayonnaise			

In a large serving bowl, layer half of lettuce, half of cauliflower and half of onion; repeat layers. Cover and chill until ready to serve. To make a dressing, combine mayonnaise, sugar and cheese. Chill until ready to serve. Just before serving, toss salad with dressing and bacon. Let sit for 5 minutes, toss again and serve immediately.

Yield: 12 to 16 servings

Chill-Out Squash Salad

¾ cup sugar
⅔ cup cider vinegar
2 tablespoons white wine vinegar
⅓ cup vegetable oil
1 teaspoon salt
½ teaspoon black pepper

Garlic salt to taste
5-10 small yellow squash, thinly sliced
1 cup chopped celery
½ cup chopped bell pepper
½ cup chopped green onion

Combine sugar, vinegars, oil, salt, black pepper and garlic salt to make a dressing. Stir until dissolved. In a large bowl, place squash, celery, bell pepper and onion. Pour dressing over vegetables and refrigerate at least 12 hours, stirring occasionally. Drain liquid from vegetables before serving, but reserve liquid to add back to any leftovers.

Yield: 6 to 8 servings

Strawberry Spinach Salad

1/2	**cup sugar**
1	**tablespoon poppy seeds**
1/2	**teaspoon minced onion**
1/4	**teaspoon paprika**
1/4	**cup cider vinegar**
1/4	**cup white vinegar**

1/4	**cup vegetable oil**
1/4	**cup olive oil**
1	**pound spinach and red leaf lettuce mixture**
1	**pint strawberries, sliced**
1/4	**cup sliced almonds, toasted**

Combine sugar, poppy seeds, onion, paprika, vinegars and oils to make a dressing. In a large bowl, combine spinach mixture, strawberries and almonds. Pour dressing over spinach mixture and toss.

Yield: 6 to 8 servings

For variety, romaine lettuce can be substituted for the red leaf lettuce and raspberry vinegar for the cider vinegar.

Woodstock Waldorf

1   (8 to 10 ounce) bag mixed salad greens
1   cup chopped dates
1   cup sugared walnuts
1   cup crumbled blue cheese

1   red or green pear, thinly sliced
    Red onion slices to taste, optional
    Poppy seed or Dijon mustard salad dressing

In a serving bowl, layer salad greens, dates, walnuts, cheese, pear and onion. Toss with salad dressing.

Yield: 6 to 8 servings

To make sugared walnuts, combine 1 cup walnuts and 6 tablespoons melted butter in a baking dish. Bake at 350° until golden brown. Immediately sprinkle with ½ cup sugar. Stir until completely coated.

Towne Lake Tortellini Salad

1	(9 ounce) package cheese tortellini noodles, cooked, drained and cooled	½	cup cubed Swiss cheese	
1	cup chopped ham	2	tablespoons minced green onion	
¾	cup frozen baby green peas, thawed	1	tablespoon minced parsley	
		2	cups Ranch salad dressing	

In a large mixing bowl, combine noodles, ham and peas. Toss gently. Add cheese, onion and parsley. Pour salad dressing over the top and mix. Cover and chill until ready to serve.

Yield: 4 to 6 servings

Curry Chicken Salad

1   cup mayonnaise
½   cup green grapes
½   cup chopped Granny Smith apple
½   teaspoon curry powder or to taste

    Black pepper
1   stalk celery, chopped
4   chicken breasts, cooked and cubed

Combine mayonnaise, grapes, apple, curry powder, pepper and celery. Stir in chicken.

Yield: 4 servings

Grammy's Chicken Salad

2½ cups chopped cooked chicken
1   cup chopped celery
1   cup pineapple chunks or tidbits
1   cup seedless grapes
½   cup nuts, toasted

1   teaspoon salt
1   teaspoon sugar
¾   teaspoon curry powder
1   cup mayonnaise
1   cup heavy cream, whipped, optional

Mix together all ingredients in order listed, carefully folding in whipped cream last.

Yield: 8 to 10 servings

This salad is great with or without whipped cream. The cream will make the salad fluffier.

Asian-Style Chicken Salad

1	cup vegetable oil	4	cups finely chopped cooked chicken
6	tablespoons rice vinegar	½	medium head cabbage, shredded (4 cups)
¼	cup sugar	¾	cup sliced almonds, toasted
½	teaspoon black pepper	1	small onion, chopped
2	(3 ounce) packages chicken-flavored ramen noodles	¼	cup sesame seeds, toasted

Whisk together oil, vinegar, sugar, pepper and seasoning packets from ramen noodles; set aside. In a large sauce-pan, bring a large amount of water to a boil. Add noodles and cook 2 to 3 minutes or until just tender. Drain and transfer noodles to a large serving bowl. Pour ¼ cup of the oil dressing mixture over the noodles. Toss to coat. Add chicken, cabbage, almonds, onion and sesame seeds to bowl. Pour remaining dressing mixture over top and toss to combine. Cover and chill 2 to 24 hours.

Yield: 8 servings

Blackberry Ketchup

1   cup red wine vinegar
1   cup water
1¾ cups brown sugar
½   teaspoon ground cloves
½   teaspoon ground ginger

1   teaspoon cinnamon
¼   teaspoon cayenne pepper
½   teaspoon salt
1   quart blackberries
1   tablespoon butter

Combine vinegar, water, sugar, cloves, ginger, cinnamon, cayenne pepper, salt and blackberries in a saucepan. Bring to a boil. Purée and strain. Whip in butter while still hot. Store in refrigerator.

Yield: 1½ quarts

This ketchup tastes great served with pork dishes. Recipe may be halved for a smaller quantity.

Featherstone's

At BridgeMill • At Towne Lake Hills

Balsamic Vinaigrette

¾	teaspoon sugar	
2	tablespoons water	
1	egg yolk	
2¼	cups olive oil	

¾	cup canola oil	
¼	cup Dijon mustard	
¾	cup balsamic vinegar	
	Salt and white pepper to taste	

In a small bowl, mix sugar and water; set aside. In a separate bowl, whisk egg yolk, oils and mustard together. Slowly whisk in sugar mixture and vinegar. Season with salt and pepper.

Yield: 1 quart

Young children, pregnant women, the elderly, and anyone with immune disorders should avoid eating raw egg.

Szechuan Peanut Dressing

1	cup smooth peanut butter
¼	cup rice wine vinegar
2¼	teaspoons chili oil
¼	cup soy sauce
	Dash of curry powder
¾	teaspoon sesame oil

3	tablespoons coconut milk
	Juice of ¼ lime
	Juice of ¼ lemon
¾	teaspoon grated fresh ginger
¾	cup water

Combine all ingredients in a food processor or blender in order listed. Blend well.

Yield: 2 cups

Asian Vinaigrette

½	teaspoon minced garlic
¼	teaspoon grated fresh ginger
¾	green onion, sliced diagonally
¼	teaspoon dry mustard
¼	teaspoon wasabi powder
1	teaspoon honey
½	tablespoon soy sauce

½	tablespoon red wine vinegar
½	teaspoon black sesame seeds
1	tablespoon fresh squeezed orange juice
1	teaspoon sesame oil
2	tablespoons canola oil
	Salt to taste

In a non-reactive bowl, whisk together garlic, ginger, onion, mustard, wasabi powder, honey, soy sauce, vinegar, sesame seeds, orange juice and salt. Slowly whisk in canola oil and sesame oil. Store in an airtight glass container.

Yield: 3 cups

Lite Honey Orange Vinaigrette

½   **cup honey**
¾   **cup orange juice**
6   **tablespoons white wine vinegar, champagne stock**
2¼ **teaspoons grated orange rind**
3¼ **shallots, chopped**

1   **tablespoon grated fresh ginger**
2   **tablespoons finely chopped fresh basil**
⅓   **cup canola oil**
⅓   **cup olive oil**

Combine honey, juice, vinegar, orange rind, shallot, ginger and basil. Whisk until blended. Gradually whisk in oils until well blended.

Yield: 2¼ cups

Featherstone's Pasta Salad

1¼	pounds dry rotini or shell pasta, cooked and drained
½	cup diced red onion
½	cup diced red bell pepper
½	cup diced green bell pepper
1	cup canned chopped tomatoes with juice
¼	cup reconstituted sun-dried tomatoes
2	tablespoons chopped garlic in oil
1	cup shredded Parmesan or Asiago cheese
½	cup crumbled feta cheese
½	cup sliced andouille sausage
2	tablespoons chopped fresh basil
	Salt and pepper to taste
⅓	cup extra virgin olive oil, or more as needed
⅓	cup balsamic vinegar, or more as needed

Combine pasta, onion, bell peppers, tomatoes, garlic, cheeses, sausage, basil, salt and pepper. Add oil and vinegar and toss. Add more oil and vinegar in equal amounts as needed to achieve desired taste.

Yield: 20 servings

Salad can be made ahead and refrigerated. Add more oil and vinegar if needed before serving. Add other blanched or raw vegetables, such as squash, carrots and green tomatoes for variety.

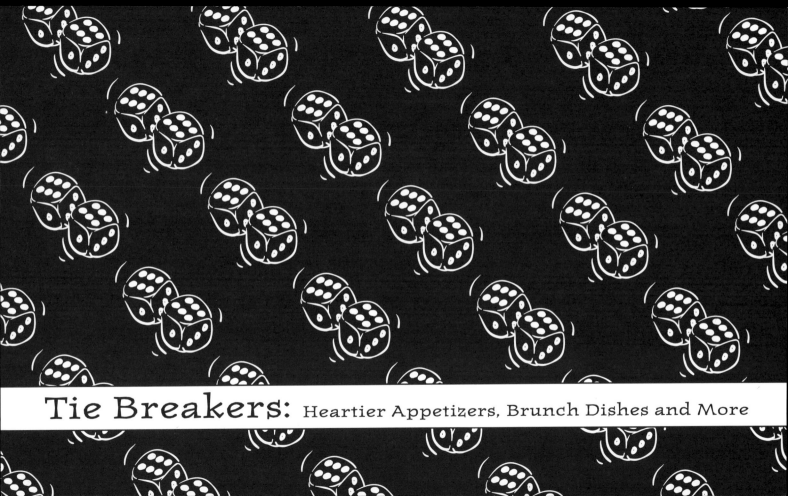

Tie Breakers: Heartier Appetizers, Brunch Dishes and More

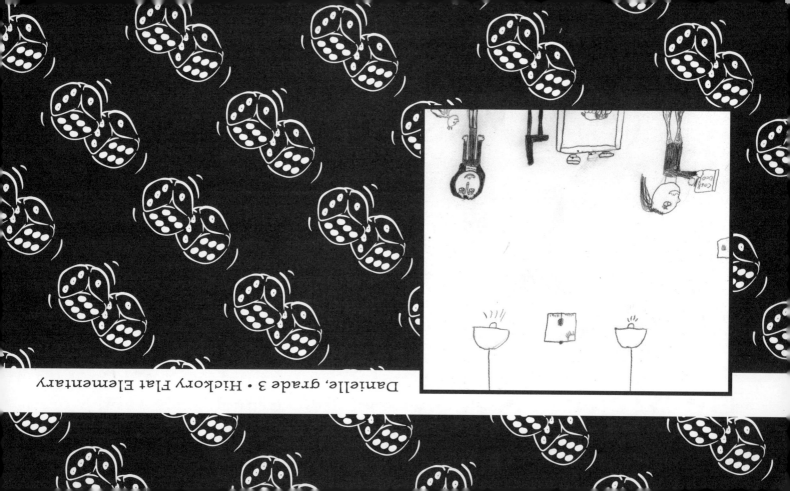

Thai Chicken on a Skewer

½ cup fresh lime juice
⅓ cup soy sauce
¼ cup brown sugar
2 tablespoons crushed red pepper flakes

4 cloves garlic, crushed
2 pounds boneless, skinless chicken breasts, cut into strips
Peanut Sauce (recipe below)

Soak bamboo skewers in cold water for 1 hour. Combine lime juice, soy sauce, sugar, pepper flakes and garlic in a bowl. Mix well. Skewer chicken onto bamboo skewers and place in a large greased glass baking dish. Pour lime juice mixture over chicken skewers and cover. Marinate in refrigerator for 6 to 10 hours. Preheat oven to 375°. Drain and discard the marinade. Bake at 375° for 30 minutes or until cooked through. Serve with Peanut Sauce.

Yield: 4 to 6 servings

Peanut Sauce

¼ cup chunky peanut butter
⅓ cup soy sauce
4 cloves garlic, minced
½ cup fresh lime juice

¼ cup coconut milk
Crushed red pepper flakes to taste
1 teaspoon paprika
1 teaspoon peanut oil

Combine peanut butter, soy sauce, garlic, lime juice, coconut milk, pepper flakes and paprika in a small saucepan. Mix well. Cook and stir until heated through, stirring constantly. Remove from heat. Stir in oil.

Yield: 1⅓ cups

Marinated Chicken Wings

3	pounds chicken drumettes	1	cup dark brown sugar
1	cup soy sauce	2	tablespoons garlic powder

Place drumettes in a large glass baking dish. In a medium bowl, combine sugar, soy sauce and garlic powder. Mix well and pour over chicken. Cover and refrigerate 24 hours. When ready to bake, preheat oven to 350°. Bake chicken, at 350°, for 20 minutes. Drain off marinade and transfer drumettes to a large baking sheet. Just before serving, preheat broiler. Broil drumettes for 5 minutes. Turn chicken and broil on other side 5 minutes longer or until chicken reaches desired crispness. Arrange on a serving platter and serve hot with plenty of napkins.

Yield: 6 to 10 servings

Baked Chicken Fingers Italiano

3	boneless, skinless chicken breast halves	¼	teaspoon black pepper
¾	cup dry bread crumbs	¼	cup olive oil
	Italian herbs to taste	1	cup marinara sauce
¼	cup Parmesan cheese		

Preheat oven to 500°. Pound chicken slightly to flatten and cut into strips. In a shallow dish, combine crumbs, herbs, cheese and pepper. Toss to mix. Brush chicken generously with oil. Dredge chicken in crumb mixture to coat thoroughly. Place chicken on a baking sheet. Bake at 500° for 10 minutes or until golden brown. While chicken bakes, heat marinara sauce. Ladle sauce over chicken just before serving or serve sauce on the side for dipping.

Yield: 6 servings

Spicy Garlic Chicken Pizza

12	ounces boneless, skinless chicken breasts		¼	teaspoon black pepper
½	cup sliced green onion, divided		1	tablespoon cornstarch
2	cloves garlic, minced		1	(16 ounce) prebaked pizza crust
2	tablespoons rice vinegar		½	cup shredded Monterey Jack cheese
2	tablespoons soy sauce		½	cup shredded mozzarella cheese
2	tablespoons olive oil, divided		2	tablespoons pine nuts
½	teaspoon crushed red pepper flakes			

Rinse chicken, pat dry and cut into ½ inch pieces. In a large bowl, combine ¼ cup green onion, garlic, vinegar, soy sauce, 1 tablespoon oil, pepper flakes and black pepper. Add chicken and stir to coat. Marinate in refrigerator for 30 minutes. Preheat oven to 400°. Drain and reserve marinade. Heat remaining 1 tablespoon oil in a large skillet. Add chicken to skillet and sauté until no longer pink. Combine reserved marinade and cornstarch and add to skillet. Cook and stir until thickened. Spoon mixture evenly onto pizza crust. Sprinkle with cheeses. Bake at 400° for 12 minutes. Top with remaining ¼ cup green onion and pine nuts. Bake 2 minutes longer. Cut into 2 inch squares or traditional wedges.

Yield: 6 servings

Garlic Tenderloin

Per pound of beef or pork tenderloin, use the following:

¼	teaspoon salt	¼	teaspoon coarse ground black pepper	
1½	tablespoons butter, softened			
¼	teaspoon minced garlic or to taste			

Preheat oven to 400°. Combine butter, garlic, salt and pepper. Spread mixture over outside of entire tenderloin. Place on a roasting rack or pan. Bake at 400° to desired degree of doneness:

Beef: 30 to 40 minutes for 3 to 5 pounds for medium rare

Pork: 30 to 40 minutes for 3 to 5 pounds for medium

Cooking time may vary. Slice cooked meat and serve immediately.

Yield: Varies

This recipe is equally good the next day when cooked meat is sliced and served cold.

Pork Tenderloin with Mustard Sauce

PORK TENDERLOIN

¼	cup soy sauce
¼	cup cooking sherry

MUSTARD SAUCE

⅓	cup sour cream
⅓	cup mayonnaise
1	tablespoon dry mustard

2	tablespoons brown sugar
2-3	pounds pork tenderloin

1	tablespoon chopped green onion
1½	teaspoons red wine vinegar
	Salt and pepper to taste

Combine soy sauce, sherry and sugar. Pour over pork and marinate in refrigerator for several hours. When ready to bake, preheat oven to 300°. Place pork on a rack in a shallow pan, reserving marinade. Bake at 300° for 1½ hours, basting frequently with marinade. Add water to pan if needed to keep basting marinade from burning to pan. Slice and serve with mustard sauce.

To make sauce, combine sour cream, mayonnaise, mustard, onion, vinegar, salt and pepper.

Yield: 6 servings

Grilled Peppered Steak with Horseradish Sauce

1¼	pounds beef flank steak		½	cup light sour cream
1½	teaspoons cracked black pepper		2	tablespoons prepared horseradish
¼	teaspoon salt		1	tablespoon minced red onion

Preheat broiler with rack positioned 4 inches from heat. Rub both sides of steak with pepper and salt. Place steak on broiler rack and broil, turning once, for 8 minutes for rare or longer for desired degree of doneness. Transfer to a serving platter and let stand 5 minutes. To make sauce, combine sour cream, horseradish and onion in a small bowl. Thinly slice steak on the diagonal, across the grain. Serve with sauce on the side.

Yield: 4 servings

Baked Ham with Spicy Sauce

1 cup pineapple juice	**1** (6 pound) boneless, rolled fully cooked ham
¾ cup light brown sugar	Whole cloves, if desired
2 tablespoons dry mustard	**1** tablespoon lemon juice
1 teaspoon ground cloves	**1** tablespoon cornstarch
½ teaspoon nutmeg	**1** tablespoon water
½ tablespoon ginger	**½** cup raisins, optional
3 teaspoons rum extract, divided	

Combine pineapple juice, sugar, mustard, cloves, nutmeg and ginger in a saucepan. Bring to a boil. Reduce heat and simmer until sugar dissolves. Add 2 teaspoons rum extract. Pierce ham several times with a fork. Pour juice mixture over ham and marinate 4 hours, basting occasionally. Preheat oven to 325°. Transfer ham to a rack, reserving marinade. Bake at 325° for 1 hour. Remove from heat, score and stud with cloves. Increase heat to 425° and bake 30 minutes longer. Combine reserved marinade and lemon juice in a small saucepan. Blend cornstarch with water and add to marinade. Cook until thickened. Add raisins and remaining 1 teaspoon rum extract. Serve sauce with ham.

Yield: 8 to 10 servings

Stuffed French Toast

1	(16 ounce) loaf sourdough French bread, cut into 18 slices	2	cups milk	
1	(8 ounce) plus 1 (3 ounce) package cream cheese, cut into ¼ inch slices	⅓	cup maple syrup	
12	large eggs		Ground cinnamon	

Place 9 slices of bread in a single layer in the bottom of a lightly greased 9x13 inch baking dish. Top with cream cheese slices. Place remaining bread slices on top of cream cheese. In a mixing bowl, whisk together eggs, milk and syrup. Pour mixture over bread. Dust with cinnamon. Cover and refrigerate 8 hours. When ready to bake, remove from refrigerator and let stand 30 minutes. Preheat oven to 350°. Bake at 350° for 45 minutes, covering with foil after 20 minutes to prevent excess browning.

Yield: 8 servings

Cardamom Sour Cream Waffles

1	cup all-purpose flour	2	eggs
½	teaspoon salt	2	cups sour cream
2	tablespoons sugar		Fruit of choice, such as cranberry sauce or strawberries
1	teaspoon cardamom		Whipped cream

Combine flour, salt, sugar and cardamom in a medium bowl. In a separate bowl, beat eggs and sour cream until blended. Add to dry ingredients and mix well. Spread about ⅓ cup of batter in a waffle iron and cook until done. Top with fruit and whipped cream.

Yield: 3 to 4 servings

Yankee Pleaser Casserole

2	pounds bulk sausage, cooked and drained	1	(8½ ounce) package corn muffin mix
2	cups shredded cheddar cheese, divided	1¾	cups hot milk
4	eggs	1	stick butter, melted
1	cup cooked grits (2 packages instant, prepared)		

Preheat oven to 325°. Layer sausage and 1 cup cheese in the bottom of a greased 2 quart casserole dish. In a medium bowl, combine eggs, grits, muffin mix, milk and butter. Pour over sausage and cheese. Top with remaining 1 cup cheese. At this point, casserole may be refrigerated or frozen until ready to serve. Bake at 325° for 1 hour in the center of the oven.

Yield: 6 to 8 servings

Rise and Shine Oatmeal Cups

CUPS

1	**pound bulk sausage**
1	**tablespoon grated onion**
⅔	**cup dry oatmeal**

FILLING

8	**eggs, beaten**
½	**cup soft cream cheese**
2	**tablespoons chopped chives**

1	**egg white**
¼	**cup milk**

¾	**cup chopped, seeded tomato, drained**
	Salt and pepper to taste

Preheat oven to 350°. In a large bowl, combine sausage, onion, oatmeal, egg white and milk. Divide mixture evenly among 12 muffin cups. Press mixture firmly into pan, pushing up sides and indenting center to form cups. Bake at 350° for 12 to 15 minutes. Remove from pan and drain on paper towels. Keep warm.

To make filling, scramble egg in a large skillet. When almost cooked, fold in cream cheese, chives, tomato, salt and pepper and cook until done. Divide filling among sausage cups.

Yield: 12 cups

Cooked cups can be frozen to use at a later time. Prepare and add filling when ready to serve.

Weekend Breakfast Casserole

4 tablespoons butter or margarine
4 cups seasoned croutons
2 cups shredded cheddar cheese
2 cups milk

8 eggs, beaten
½ teaspoon dry mustard
1 (12 ounce) package bacon, cooked and crumbled

Preheat oven to 325°. Place butter in a 9x13 inch baking dish and melt in preheating oven. Tilt dish to coat bottom and sides. Add croutons to dish. Sprinkle cheese over croutons. In a mixing bowl, combine milk, egg and mustard. Mix well. Pour mixture over cheese and sprinkle with bacon. Bake at 325° for 40 to 50 minutes or until set. Remove from oven and let stand 5 to 10 minutes before serving.

Yield: 8 to 10 servings

Featherstone's

AT BRIDGEMILL • AT TOWNE LAKE HILLS

Quiche Base Mixture

3	(9 inch) deep-dish pie shells		2	cups half-and-half
8	eggs			Salt and pepper to taste
8	egg yolks			Cayenne pepper to taste
1	cup heavy cream			

Preheat oven to 350°. With a fork, prick bottom and sides of pie shells. Prebake shells at 350° for 5 minutes; set aside. In a large bowl, whisk together eggs, egg yolks, cream and half-and-half. Season with salt and peppers. Fill pie shells with additional ingredients of your choice. Vegetables should be partially cooked and meats should be fully cooked. Pour egg mixture into shells to cover. Bake at 350° for 45 to 60 minutes or until lightly browned.

Yield: 18 servings

Mini Sausage Melts

1 loaf sliced white bread, crust removed	½-1 stick butter
⅓ cup chopped green onion	2 tablespoons all-purpose flour
1 (4 ounce) can chopped mushrooms, drained	2 cups heavy cream
½ cup chopped black olives	¼ cup Parmesan cheese
1 pound bulk sausage, cooked and drained	

Preheat oven to 300°. Use a rolling pin to roll each bread slice to about ¼ inch thick. Cut each bread square into four squares and press each small square into a greased mini muffin cup to form a crust. Repeat until 4 muffin pans are filled. Bake at 300° for 10 minutes. In a mixing bowl, combine onion, mushrooms and olives. Mix well. Stir in sausage. Melt butter in a medium saucepan. Stir in flour and cream. Cook 10 to 15 minutes to thicken. Remove from heat and add sausage mixture. Pour into mini crusts. Top with cheese. Increase oven to 350° and bake 10 minutes.

Yield: 32 pieces

Featherstone's
AT BRIDGEMILL • AT TOWNE LAKE HILLS

Cheese Grits

9	cups half-and-half	1	cup shredded white cheddar cheese or grated
½	cube chicken bouillon		Parmesan cheese
1¼	cups quick-cooking grits		Minced garlic or pesto to taste, optional

Combine half-and-half and bouillon in a saucepan and stir to dissolve bouillon. Bring mixture to a boil. Reduce heat to low and stir in grits. Cook and stir until thickened. Add cheese. Stir in garlic or pesto, if using.

Yield: 10 to 12 servings

Chicken Tetrazzini

¼ cup chopped green bell pepper
1 medium onion, chopped
2 tablespoons butter
3-4 cups chopped cooked chicken
¼ cup chopped pimento
¼ teaspoon salt
¼ teaspoon black pepper

¼ teaspoon celery salt
2 cups condensed cream of mushroom soup
3 cups shredded cheddar cheese
1 (14½ ounce) can chicken broth
1 (4 ounce) can sliced mushrooms
1 (8 ounce) package thin spaghetti, cooked and drained
Paprika

Preheat oven to 350°. Sauté bell pepper and onion in butter. Combine sautéed vegetables, chicken, pimento, salt, pepper, celery salt, soup, cheese, broth and mushrooms in a large bowl. Stir in spaghetti. Mix well and transfer to a greased 9x13 inch casserole dish. Sprinkle with paprika. Cover and bake at 350° for 45 to 60 minutes.

Yield: 10 to 12 servings

Classic Cheesy Lasagna

1	pound bulk Italian sausage
1/2	cup chopped onion
1	clove garlic, minced
2	(8 ounce) cans tomato sauce, divided
2	(6 ounce) cans tomato paste
1/2	cup hot water
1	teaspoon basil
1	teaspoon oregano
1/2	teaspoon marjoram

1	(16 ounce) container ricotta cheese
1	(10 ounce) package frozen chopped spinach, thawed and well-drained
1/2	cup grated Parmesan cheese
3	eggs
1/2	teaspoon salt
1/2	(16-ounce) package lasagna noodles, cooked and drained
2	cups shredded mozzarella cheese
2	cups shredded Muenster cheese

Preheat oven to 350˚. In a medium skillet, combine sausage, onion and garlic. Cook and stir until no longer pink; drain. Reserve ⅔ cup tomato sauce. Stir remaining tomato sauce, tomato paste, water, basil, oregano and marjoram into sausage mixture. Bring to a boil. Reduce heat and simmer 5 minutes. In a medium bowl, combine ricotta cheese, spinach, Parmesan cheese, eggs and salt. Mix well. Spread reserved tomato sauce in the bottom of a 9x13 inch pan. Layer one-third of each: noodles, ricotta mixture, meat mixture, mozzarella cheese and Muenster cheese. Repeat layers twice. Bake, uncovered, at 350˚ for 40 to 50 minutes or until hot and bubbly. Let stand 5 to 10 minutes before cutting.

Yield: 12 servings

Razorback Casserole

1   **(8 ounce) package wide egg noodles**
1   **(16 ounce) container sour cream**
1   **(8 ounce) package cream cheese, cubed and softened**

2   **(15½ ounce) jars spaghetti sauce with meat**
4   **cups shredded cheddar cheese**

Preheat oven to 350°. Cook noodles according to package directions. Drain and transfer hot noodles to a large mixing bowl. While noodles are still hot, add sour cream and cream cheese to bowl and stir until blended. Place a small amount of spaghetti sauce in the bottom of a greased 9x13 inch pan. Add a layer of noodle mixture, then a layer of sauce and a layer of cheddar cheese. Repeat layers, ending with a generous amount of cheddar cheese. Bake at 350° for 20 to 30 minutes.

Yield: 8 to 10 servings

An equivalent amount of homemade spaghetti sauce with meat can be used in place of the store-bought, if desired.

El Grando

1	(10 ounce) package yellow rice, cooked	1	cup shredded cheddar cheese
1	pound ground beef		Chopped onion, lettuce, tomato and Spanish olives as desired
1	(1¼ ounce) package dry taco seasoning		Crushed corn chips and sour cream for garnish
1	(14½ ounce) can diced tomatoes, undrained		

Place cooked rice in a 9x13 inch casserole dish. In a skillet, brown beef; drain. Stir in taco seasoning and tomatoes. Simmer 15 minutes. Pour mixture over rice and sprinkle with cheese. Top with onion, lettuce, tomato and olives. Garnish each serving with corn chips and a dollop of sour cream.

Yield: 8 to 12 servings

The base casserole, not including onion, lettuce, tomato, olives or garnishes, will keep for several days in the refrigerator. Microwave when ready to serve and add extras when warm.

Best-Ever Sloppy Joes

1 pound ground beef
1 medium onion, chopped
¼ cup chopped green bell pepper
1 cup ketchup
2 teaspoons prepared mustard

2 tablespoons white vinegar
2 tablespoons sugar
2 tablespoons Worcestershire sauce
1 cup water or as needed

Cook beef, onion and bell pepper in a skillet until meat is brown and vegetables are tender; drain. Add ketchup, mustard, vinegar, sugar and Worcestershire sauce. Mix well. Gradually add as much water as needed to reach desired thickness. Simmer 20 to 30 minutes.

Yield: 6 to 8 servings

This versatile recipe can be served from a chafing dish and spooned onto cocktail rolls as an hors d'oeuvre or piled onto hamburger buns from a crockpot for a casual tailgate party. These Sloppy Joes will keep for several days in the refrigerator or can be frozen and reheated in the microwave. The recipe easily doubles for a crowd.

Apple Sensation

1	stick butter or margarine
2	apples, peeled and sliced
6	eggs
½	cup milk
1	cup all-purpose flour

3	tablespoons granulated sugar
1	tablespoon vanilla
½	teaspoon salt
¼	teaspoon cinnamon
2-3	tablespoons brown sugar

Preheat oven to 425°. Melt butter in a 9x13 inch pan by placing in oven. Add apples to pan and return to oven until butter sizzles. In a medium bowl, beat eggs. Stir in milk, flour, granulated sugar, vanilla, salt and cinnamon. Pour mixture over apples. Sprinkle with brown sugar. Bake at 425° for 20 minutes.

Yield: 16 servings

Scalloped Pineapples

1	stick butter or margarine, melted	1	cup sugar
4	cups fresh bread cubes (about 6 slices)	½	cup evaporated milk
3	eggs	1	(20 ounce) can crushed pineapple, undrained

Preheat oven to 350°. Combine butter and bread cubes; set aside. In a large mixing bowl, beat together eggs, sugar and milk. Add bread cubes and stir well. Mix in pineapple. Pour into an ungreased 2 quart baking dish. Bake, uncovered, at 350° for 1 hour.

Yield: 8 servings

Canned cherries, fresh strawberries or apples and raisins can be substituted for the pineapple.

Pretty in Pink Salad

1	(16 ounce) container frozen whipped topping, thawed	1	(20 ounce) can crushed pineapple, drained
1	(14 ounce) can sweetened condensed milk	1	cup chopped nuts, optional
1	(21 ounce) can cherry pie filling		

In a large bowl, fold together whipped topping, milk and pie filling until well blended. Stir in pineapple and nuts. Pour into a 9x13 inch dish and freeze. Remove from freezer 30 minutes before serving. Serve on a bed of lettuce, if desired.

Yield: 16 servings

Strawberry Pretzel Salad

CRUST

2	cups crushed pretzels
1½	sticks butter, melted
1	tablespoon sugar

FILLING

1	(12 ounce) container frozen whipped topping, thawed
1	(8 ounce) package cream cheese, softened
1	cup sugar

TOPPING

2	(3-ounce) packages strawberry jello
1	(10 ounce) package frozen sliced sweetened strawberries, thawed

Preheat oven to 450°. Combine pretzels, butter and sugar and press into a 9x13 inch pan. Bake at 450° for 10 minutes. Cool.

To prepare filling, use an electric mixer on medium speed to mix whipped topping, cream cheese and sugar until smooth. Spread filling over cooled crust.

For topping, prepare jello according to package directions. Stir in strawberries. Refrigerate until thickened but not set. Spoon over filling and refrigerate until set.

Yield: 10 to 12 servings

Cloud Nine Salad

SALAD

1 (¼ ounce) package unflavored gelatin
¼ cup cold water
1 cup boiling water
⅔ cup sugar

1 teaspoon vanilla
1 (16 ounce) container sour cream
1 (8 ounce) container frozen whipped topping, thawed

SAUCE

1 (4¾ ounce) package strawberry or raspberry Junket Danish Dessert Pudding and Pie Filling Glaze mix

2½ cups cold water
1 (10 ounce) container frozen strawberries or raspberries, thawed

Dissolve gelatin in cold water. Add boiling water and stir until dissolved. Add sugar and vanilla and stir until dissolved. Whisk in sour cream until smooth. Whisk in whipped topping. Pour into a 6 cup mold or a clear glass bowl. Refrigerate overnight.

To make sauce, combine pudding mix and cold water in a medium saucepan. Bring to a boil. Boil and stir constantly for 1 minute. Cool slightly. Fold in strawberries. Unmold salad onto a serving plate. Pour sauce over salad or serve sauce on the side.

Yield: 12 servings

Junket pudding mix can be found in the ice-cream topping section of your local grocery store. Other fruit glaze can be substituted.

For easy release of salad from mold, dip bottom of mold in warm water for 1 minute.

Hash Brown Cheesy Potatoes

1	(10¾ ounce) can condensed cream of celery soup
1	(10¾ ounce) can condensed cream of chicken soup
1	(8 ounce) container sour cream
½	cup chopped onion, optional
1	stick butter, melted
2	cups shredded cheese
1	teaspoon salt
1	teaspoon black pepper
1	(32 ounce) package frozen cubed or shredded potatoes

Preheat oven to 350°. In a large bowl, combine soups, sour cream, butter, cheese, salt and pepper. Stir in potatoes. Spread mixture in an ungreased 9x13 inch baking dish. Bake at 350° for 1½ hours.

Yield: 8 servings

Custard Corn

1	cup milk
2	eggs, beaten
½	teaspoon salt
1	tablespoon cornstarch
2	tablespoons sugar
½	teaspoon black pepper
2	cups canned corn, well drained (do not use frozen)
4	tablespoons butter, melted

Preheat oven to 350°. Combine milk, egg, salt, cornstarch, sugar and pepper. Blend well. Stir in corn and butter. Pour into a 2 quart casserole dish. Bake at 350° for 1 hour.

Yield: 6 servings

Match Point: Desserts That Hit the Sweet Spot

Christina, grade 5 • Woodstock Elementary

Melt-A-Way Sugar Cookies

1	cup vegetable oil	1	teaspoon salt
2	sticks butter	1	teaspoon cream of tartar
1	cup sugar	1	teaspoon baking soda
2	eggs	4	cups all-purpose flour
1	teaspoon vanilla		Colored or granulated sugar for dipping glass

Preheat oven to 350°. Cream oil, butter and sugar until light and fluffy. Mix in eggs. Add vanilla, salt, cream of tartar and baking soda. Mix well. Gradually mix in flour until all ingredients are well blended. Drop by spoonfuls onto an ungreased baking sheet. Press dough flat using the bottom of a glass that has been greased and then dipped in sugar. Bake at 350° for 10 minutes.

Yield: 6 dozen

No Bake Peanut Butter Cookies

½	cup corn syrup, honey or molasses	1	cup peanut butter
½	cup sugar	2	cups Special K cereal

Bring syrup and sugar to a boil in a heavy saucepan. Remove from heat. Stir in peanut butter until well blended. Mix in cereal. Drop by spoonfuls onto wax paper. Cool.

Yield: 2 dozen

Neiman Marcus Cookies

4	sticks butter
2	cups sugar
2	cups brown sugar
4	eggs
2	teaspoons vanilla
4	cups all-purpose flour
5	cups dry oatmeal, powdered

1	teaspoon salt
2	teaspoons baking powder
2	teaspoons baking soda
1	(24 ounce) package chocolate chips
3	cups chopped nuts
1	(8 ounce) chocolate candy bar, grated

Preheat oven to 375°. Cream butter and sugars. Mix in eggs and vanilla. In a separate bowl, combine flour, oatmeal, salt, baking powder and baking soda. Blend dry ingredients into creamed mixture. Stir in chocolate chips, nuts and grated chocolate. Roll into balls and place 2 inches apart on a baking sheet. Bake at 375° for 10 minutes.

Yield: 9 dozen

This recipe can be easily halved.

For powdered oatmeal, process 5 cups of dry oatmeal in a blender until it is a fine powder.

Swiss Chocolate Cookies

1   (18¼ ounce) package Swiss chocolate cake mix
2   eggs
½   cup oil

1   cup semi-sweet chocolate chips
2   cups chopped pecans

Preheat oven to 350°. Combine cake mix, eggs and oil by hand in a mixing bowl. Fold in chocolate chips and pecans. Drop by spoonfuls onto an ungreased baking sheet. Bake at 350° for 10 to 12 minutes.

Yield: 2 to 3 dozen

Fudge Nut Cookies

1   stick butter
1   (12 ounce) package semi-sweet chocolate chips
1   (14 ounce) can sweetened condensed milk

1   teaspoon vanilla
1   cup flour
1   cup chopped nuts

Preheat oven to 350°. Heat butter, chocolate and milk in a saucepan until melted. Remove from heat and stir in vanilla. Mix in flour and nuts. Drop by spoonfuls onto a lightly greased baking sheet. Bake at 350° for 7 to 8 minutes.

Yield: 3 dozen

White Chocolate Macadamia Nut Cookies

1	stick butter or margarine, softened	2	cups all-purpose flour	
½	cup shortening	1	teaspoon baking soda	
¾	cup brown sugar	½	teaspoon salt	
½	cup granulated sugar	1	(6 ounce) package white baking chocolate, chopped	
1	egg	1	(7 ounce) jar macadamia nuts, coarsely chopped	
1½	teaspoons vanilla			

Preheat oven to 350°. Cream butter and shortening until fluffy using an electric mixer on medium speed. Gradually add sugars, beating well. Mix in egg and vanilla. In a separate bowl, combine flour, baking soda and salt. Gradually add dry ingredients to creamed mixture. Beat well. Stir in chocolate and nuts. Drop by rounded teaspoonfuls, 2 inches apart, onto a lightly greased baking sheet. Bake at 350° until done.

Yield: 2 to 3 dozen

Tennis Bars

1   (18¼ ounce) package yellow cake mix
3   eggs, divided
1   stick butter, melted

1   cup chopped pecans
1   (8 ounce) package cream cheese, softened
1   (16 ounce) package powdered sugar

Preheat oven to 325°. Combine cake mix, 1 egg and butter until mixed. Stir in pecans. Press into a greased 9x13 inch nonstick pan. Blend cream cheese, sugar and remaining 2 eggs together. Spread mixture over cake mixture. Bake at 325° for 35 to 40 minutes. Cool before cutting into squares.

Yield: 20 to 24 servings

Great for tennis matches; your opponents will love them. Can be made a day ahead or frozen.

Cookie Treat Bars

2	sticks butter or margarine		1/2	teaspoon baking powder
1	cup granulated sugar		2	cups all-purpose flour
1	cup brown sugar		1/2	teaspoon salt
2	eggs, beaten		2	cups dry oatmeal
1	teaspoon vanilla		1	(12 ounce) package chocolate chips
1	teaspoon baking soda			

Preheat oven to 325°. Cream butter and sugars together. Mix in eggs and vanilla. In a separate bowl, combine baking soda, baking powder, flour and salt. Stir oatmeal and then chocolate chips into dry ingredients. Mix dry ingredients into creamed mixture. Spread into a 12x18x1 inch baking pan. Bake at 325° for 20 to 25 minutes. Cool before cutting into bars.

Yield: 16 servings

Cherry Cheese Cake Bars

CRUST

1¼ cups all-purpose flour
½ cup brown sugar
½ cup butter flavored shortening

½ cup finely chopped walnuts
½ cup flaked coconut

FILLING

2 (8 ounce) packages cream cheese, softened
⅔ cup granulated sugar
2 eggs

2 teaspoons vanilla
1 (21 ounce) can cherry pie filling
½ cup coarsely chopped walnuts

Preheat oven to 350°. Combine flour and sugar in a mixing bowl. Cut in shortening until mixture resembles fine crumbs. Add walnuts and coconut. Mix well. Reserve ½ cup of mixture and press remaining mixture into a greased 9x13 inch baking pan. Bake at 350° for 12 to 15 minutes or until edges are lightly browned.

To make filling, beat together cream cheese, sugar, eggs and vanilla until smooth. Spread over hot crust. Return to oven and bake 15 minutes longer. Spread pie filling over cheese layer. Combine reserved ½ cup crust mixture and walnuts and sprinkle over filling. Bake another 15 minutes. Cool and then refrigerate several hours. Cut into bars.

Yield: 20 to 24 servings

Glazed Spice Bars

BARS

¾	cup vegetable oil
¼	cup honey
1	cup granulated sugar
1	egg

GLAZE

1	cup powdered sugar
1	teaspoon vanilla

2	cups self-rising flour
1	teaspoon cinnamon
1	cup chopped pecans

1	tablespoon mayonnaise
1	tablespoon water

Preheat oven to 350°. To prepare bars, combine oil, honey, sugar, egg, flour, cinnamon and pecans in a mixing bowl. Mix well. Dough will be stiff. Press into a 9x13 inch baking pan. Bake at 350° for 25 to 40 minutes. Meanwhile, make a glaze by mixing together powdered sugar, vanilla, mayonnaise and water. Pour glaze over top of baked bars while still hot.

Yield: 20 to 24 servings

Pumpkin Bars

BARS

4	eggs
1⅔	cups sugar
1	cup oil
1	(16 ounce) can pumpkin

2	cups flour
2	teaspoons baking powder
2	teaspoons cinnamon
1	teaspoon salt
1	teaspoon baking soda

FROSTING

1	(3 ounce) package cream cheese, softened
1	teaspoon vanilla

2	cups powdered sugar

Preheat oven to 350°. Beat together eggs, sugar, oil and pumpkin. In a separate bowl, combine flour, baking powder, cinnamon, salt and baking soda. Mix dry ingredients into pumpkin mixture. Spread batter in a greased 10x15x1 inch baking pan. Bake at 350° for 25 to 30 minutes. Cool. To prepare frosting, combine cream cheese, vanilla and powdered sugar. Spread over cooled bars.

Yield: 15 to 18 servings

Toffee Brownie Bars

1½	sticks butter or margarine, softened		1½	cups all-purpose flour
¾	cup brown sugar		1	(20 ounce) package fudge brownie mix
1	egg yolk		1	(12 ounce) package milk chocolate chips, melted
¾	teaspoon vanilla		¾	cup finely chopped pecans

Preheat oven to 350°. Combine butter, sugar, egg yolk and vanilla in a large bowl. Stir in flour. Spread mixture in a greased 10½x15½ inch baking pan. Bake at 350° for 15 minutes or until golden. Meanwhile, prepare brownie mix according to package directions. Spread brownie filling over hot crust. Bake 15 minutes longer or until surface appears set. Cool 30 minutes. Spread chocolate over filling and sprinkle with pecans. Cool completely in pan on a wire rack.

Yield: 4 dozen

Snickers Brownies

1   (14 ounce) can sweetened condensed milk, divided
1   (18¼ ounce) package German chocolate cake mix
1½ cups salted peanuts

1   stick butter or margarine, melted
1   (14 ounce) package caramels
1½ cups chocolate chips

Preheat oven to 350°. Reserve ⅓ cup plus 2 tablespoons condensed milk. Mix remaining milk, cake mix, peanuts and butter in a large bowl. Spread or crumble half of mixture in the bottom of a greased 9x13 inch baking pan; set aside remaining mixture. Bake at 350° for 6 to 8 minutes or until mixture is soft. Meanwhile, combine caramels and reserved condensed milk in a microwave-safe bowl. Microwave on high for 2 to 3 minutes or until melted, stirring occasionally to prevent burning. Keep warm until ready to use. Remove brownies from oven and sprinkle with chocolate chips. Working quickly, use a large spatula to spread warm caramel over chips. Crumble remaining cake mixture on top. Press with a spoon to set. Bake 18 to 20 minutes longer or until brownies separate from sides of pan. Do not overbake to prevent caramel from hardening. Cool and cut into 1½ inch pieces.

Yield: 48 servings

These brownies are fairly rich, a 1½ inch piece goes a long way.

Rocky Road Brownies

1	(20 ounce) package walnut brownie mix		1	stick butter, softened
3	cups mini marshmallows		½	teaspoon vanilla
2	ounces unsweetened chocolate, melted		1	(1 pound) package powdered sugar
⅓	cup milk			

Prepare brownies as directed on package. Immediately after removing from oven, scatter marshmallows on top. Make an icing by combining chocolate, milk and butter in a bowl. Mix well. Stir in vanilla and powdered sugar. Drizzle icing over marshmallows. Cool and chill before cutting.

Yield: 24 servings

If desired, substitute 6 tablespoons cocoa plus 2 tablespoons butter for the unsweetened chocolate.

Cream Cheese Brownies

2	(3 ounce) packages cream cheese, softened		2	tablespoons all-purpose flour
5	tablespoons butter, softened		¾	teaspoon vanilla
⅓	cup sugar		1	(20 ounce) package brownie mix, with or without nuts
2	eggs		1	(16 ounce) can chocolate frosting

Preheat oven to 350°. Beat cream cheese and butter together. Add sugar, eggs, flour and vanilla. Beat until smooth. Set aside. Prepare brownie mix according to package directions. Spread half of brownie batter in a greased 9x13 inch baking pan. Pour cream cheese mixture over batter. Spoon remaining batter over cream cheese mixture. Swirl cream cheese and top brownie layers together with a knife. Bake at 350° for 35 to 38 minutes. Cool before spreading frosting over top.

Yield: 24 servings

Easy Microwave Fudge

1	(1 pound) package powdered sugar		1	stick margarine
⅓	cup cocoa		1	teaspoon vanilla
¼	cup milk		½	cup chopped pecans

Combine sugar, cocoa, milk and margarine in a microwavable bowl. Microwave on high for 2 minutes. Add vanilla and pecans and mix well. Pour mixture into a foil- or wax paper-lined pan. Freeze 20 minutes. Transfer to refrigerator and chill overnight.

Yield: 24 pieces

Lazy Woman's Fudge

1	(7 ounce) jar marshmallow creme	1	(12 ounce) package milk chocolate chips
1½	cups sugar	1	(6 ounce) package semi-sweet chocolate chips
⅔	cup evaporated milk	1	teaspoon vanilla
4	tablespoons butter	¼	teaspoon salt

Combine marshmallow creme, sugar, milk, butter and salt in a heavy saucepan. Bring to a boil. Cook and stir 5 minutes. Remove from heat and stir in both types of chocolate chips until melted. Add vanilla. Pour into a foil-lined 8 inch square pan. Chill about 2 hours or until firm.

Yield: 10 servings

Peanut Butter Balls

1	(18 ounce) jar peanut butter (2 cups)	1	stick margarine, softened
1	(1 pound) package powdered sugar	12-24	ounces semi-sweet chocolate
1	teaspoon vanilla		Dash of vegetable oil

Combine peanut butter, sugar, vanilla and margarine. Roll into small balls and place on wax paper. Cover and freeze 24 hours for best results. Melt chocolate in the top of a double boiler. Thin as needed (1 tablespoon at the most) with oil. Stirring chocolate frequently, dip balls in chocolate with a spoon. Return balls to wax paper and freeze until ready to serve.

Yield: 3 dozen

Peanut butter mixture can be shaped like eggs and then dipped in chocolate for a springtime treat. Yield: 2 dozen

Black Bottoms

DARK BATTER

1½	cups all-purpose flour
1	cup sugar
¼	cup cocoa
½	teaspoon salt
1	teaspoon baking soda

LIGHT BATTER

1	egg
⅓	cup sugar
⅛	teaspoon salt

1	cup water
½	cup vegetable oil
1	tablespoon vinegar
1	teaspoon vanilla

1	(8 ounce) package cream cheese, softened
1	(12 ounce) package chocolate chips

Preheat oven to 350°. To make dark batter, combine flour, sugar, cocoa, salt and baking soda in a large bowl. Add water, oil, vinegar and vanilla. Beat until smooth.

For light batter, combine egg, sugar, salt, cream cheese and chocolate chips in a small bowl. Mix by hand until thoroughly blended.

In 80 mini muffin papers, place 1 teaspoon dark batter and ½ teaspoon light batter. Bake at 350° for 20 minutes.

Yield: 80 pieces

Pecan Tassies

CRUST

1 stick margarine
1 (3 ounce) package cream cheese

1 cup all-purpose flour

FILLING

1 egg, beaten
¾ cup brown sugar
½ cup ground pecans

1 teaspoon margarine, melted
½ teaspoon vanilla

Preheat oven to 350°. To prepare crust, combine margarine, cream cheese and flour. Form into 1 inch balls and press into small muffin tins, pushing up the sides to make a shell. Combine egg, sugar, pecans, margarine and vanilla to make filling. Spoon into crust shells, filling two-thirds full. Bake at 350° for 20 to 25 minutes.

Yield: 2 dozen

Chocolate Chess Pie

1	stick butter	3	eggs
1½	cups sugar	1	teaspoon vanilla
2	rounded tablespoons cocoa	¼	cup milk
1	rounded tablespoon flour	1	pie crust, unbaked

Preheat oven to 350°. Melt butter in a saucepan. In a small mixing bowl, combine sugar, cocoa and flour. Mix well and add to saucepan. Add eggs one at a time, stirring after each addition. Stir in vanilla and milk. Pour mixture into crust. Bake at 350° for 40 minutes.

Yield: 8 servings

Bama "Roll Tide" Chess Pie

1	cup sugar	1	tablespoon distilled vinegar
3	eggs, beaten	1	tablespoon vanilla
6	tablespoons butter or margarine, melted	1	pie crust, unbaked

Preheat oven to 325°. Combine sugar, egg and butter. Add vinegar and vanilla and mix well. Pour into pie crust. Bake at 325° for 45 to 60 minutes.

Yield: 8 servings

Kentucky Hi Pie

2	eggs	1½	cups sugar
1	stick margarine, melted	1	teaspoon vanilla
½	cup cornstarch	1	cup chocolate chips
1	cup nuts	1	pie crust, unbaked

Preheat oven to 350°. Combine eggs, margarine, cornstarch, nuts, sugar, vanilla and chocolate chips. Pour mixture into pie crust. Bake at 350° for 45 minutes. Serve topped with ice cream or whipped cream.

Yield: 8 servings

Do not cut back on the sugar as the recipe will not be as good.

Quick and Easy Fudge Pie

1	stick butter or margarine		Pinch of salt
¼	cup cocoa	¼	cup flour
1	cup sugar	1	teaspoon vanilla
2	eggs, beaten		

Preheat oven to 300°. Melt butter in a saucepan. Stir in cocoa, sugar, eggs, salt, flour and vanilla. Mix well. Pour into a greased round cake pan. Bake at 300° for 30 minutes. Serve warm topped with vanilla ice cream.

Yield: 6 to 8 servings

Frozen Margarita Pie

1½	cups finely crushed pretzel crumbs	¼	cup fresh lime juice
1	stick butter, melted	3	tablespoons tequila
½	cup sugar	2	tablespoons triple sec
1	(14 ounce) can sweetened condensed milk	1	cup heavy cream, whipped

Combine crumbs, butter and sugar. Press firmly into bottom and up sides of a lightly greased 9 inch pie plate. In a large bowl, combine milk, juice, tequila and triple sec. Mix well. Fold in whipped cream. Pour into crust. Freeze until firm. Remove from freezer 10 minutes prior to serving. Garnish with lime zest curls.

Yield: 6 to 8 servings

Tequila and triple sec may be cut back to suit taste.

Easy Key Lime Pie

4 egg yolks
1 (14 ounce) can sweetened condensed milk
1 (8 ounce) package cream cheese, cubed and softened
⅔ cup key lime juice
1 graham cracker crust

Preheat oven to 350°. Combine egg yolks and milk. Mix well. Blend in cream cheese, 1 cube at a time. Slowly mix in lime juice. Stir until smooth and creamy. Pour mixture into crust. Bake at 350° for 10 minutes. Chill. Serve topped with whipped cream and garnished with lime slices.

Yield: 8 servings

Girdle Buster Pie

2 pints coffee ice cream
1 chocolate graham cracker pie crust
1 (16 ounce) jar hot fudge
Chocolate sandwich cookies, optional

Soften ice cream in a large bowl. Crumble pie crust over ice cream. Add fudge and mix well. Spoon mixture into individual serving dishes. Freeze. Crumble cookies on top before serving.

Yield: 6 to 10 servings

Use 1 quart of ice cream and 2 pie crusts. Layer ice cream, crust and fudge in a 9x13 inch pan instead of mixing ingredients together.

Fruit Cocktail Pie

1	cup flour	1	(15¼ ounce) can fruit cocktail, drained
1	cup sugar	½	cup chopped nuts
½	teaspoon salt	3	tablespoons brown sugar
1	teaspoon baking soda		Whipped cream
1	egg, lightly beaten		

Preheat oven to 350°. Combine flour, sugar, salt and baking soda in a large bowl. Add fruit cocktail and mix until thoroughly blended. Pour into a well greased 9 or 10 inch pie pan. Sprinkle nuts and sugar over top. Bake at 350° for 30 to 45 minutes or until golden brown on top. Serve topped with whipped cream.

Yield: 6 to 8 servings

This pie makes its own crust as it bakes.

Irene's Millionaire Pie

1   **(14 ounce) can sweetened condensed milk**
2   **tablespoons lemon juice**
1   **(8 ounce) container frozen whipped topping, thawed**
1   **(15 ounce) can crushed pineapple, well drained**

1   **cup chopped pecans**
2   **graham cracker pie crusts**
   Crushed pecans

Combine milk and juice. Blend well. Fold in whipped topping, pineapple and chopped pecans. Divide mixture between pie crusts. Freeze. Serve topped with crushed pecans.

Yield: 2 pies, 8 servings each

Everyone's Favorite Cobbler

1   **stick butter**
1   **cup self-rising flour**
1   **cup sugar**

1   **cup milk**
2   **cups fresh or frozen fruit of choice or combination of fruits**
⅛   **cup liquid from fruit**

Preheat oven to 325°. While preheating, melt butter in oven in a 2 quart casserole dish. In a mixing bowl, combine flour and sugar. Slowly mix in milk; set aside. Place fruit in casserole dish; do not stir. Pour fruit liquid into casserole dish. Pour milk mixture over fruit. Bake at 325° for 40 to 45 minutes.

Yield: 8 servings

Sour Cream Pound Cake

2	sticks butter	1/4	teaspoon baking soda
3	cups sugar	3	cups sifted flour
6	eggs, separated	1	cup sour cream

Preheat oven to 300°. Cream butter and sugar thoroughly in a large bowl. Add egg yolks, one at a time. Mix together baking soda and flour and add to creamed mixture alternately with sour cream. In a separate bowl, beat egg whites until stiff. Fold whites into batter. Pour batter into a greased and floured 10 inch tube pan. Bake at 300° for 1¼ to 2 hours or until a toothpick inserted in center of cake comes out clean. Cake will be nicely browned on top. Let stand 15 minutes before removing from pan.

Yield: 12 to 16 servings

Peach Crisp

1	(29 ounce) can sliced peaches, undrained	1	cup chopped nuts
1	(18¼ ounce) package yellow cake mix	1	cup shredded coconut
1	stick butter, melted		

Preheat oven to 350°. Place undrained peaches in a 9x13 inch baking pan. Sprinkle cake mix over peaches. Pour butter over top. Sprinkle with nuts and coconut. Bake at 350° for 50 to 60 minutes. Serve with vanilla ice cream.

Yield: 12 servings

Peaches-N-Cream

¾ cup all-purpose flour
1 (3.9 ounce) package vanilla pudding mix
1 teaspoon baking powder
1 egg, beaten
½ cup milk

3 tablespoons butter, melted
1 (16 ounce) can sliced peaches, drained, juice reserved
1 (8 ounce) package cream cheese, cubed and softened
½ cup plus 1 tablespoon sugar, divided
½ teaspoon cinnamon

Preheat oven to 350°. Combine flour, pudding mix and baking powder in a mixing bowl. In a separate bowl, combine egg, milk and butter. Stir milk mixture into dry ingredients. Mix well. Spread batter in a greased 8 inch square baking pan. Chop peaches and sprinkle over batter. Beat together ⅓ cup of reserved peach juice, cream cheese, and ½ cup sugar. Pour mixture over peaches. Sprinkle remaining 1 tablespoon sugar and cinnamon on top. Bake at 350° for 45 minutes. Serve warm.

Yield: 8 to 9 servings

Apple Pound Cake

1½	cups vegetable oil		4	cups diced apple
2	cups granulated sugar		1	cup chopped walnuts
3	eggs		2	teaspoons vanilla
3	cups all-purpose flour		1	stick butter
1	teaspoon salt		½	cup brown sugar
1	teaspoon baking soda		2	tablespoons brandy or vanilla
1½	teaspoons cinnamon			

Preheat oven to 350°. Combine oil, granulated sugar, eggs, flour, salt, baking soda and cinnamon in a large bowl. Mix until smooth. Fold in apple, walnuts and vanilla. Pour batter into a greased and floured 10 inch tube pan or three 9x5 inch loaf pans. Bake at 350° for 1 hour, 20 minutes. Cool 20 minutes before removing from pan. Meanwhile, prepare a glaze by melting butter in a medium saucepan. Stir in brown sugar and brandy. Bring to a boil and cook 2 minutes. Invert cake onto a serving plate. Spoon glaze over top.

Yield: 8 to 12 servings

Coconut Pound Cake

CAKE

5   eggs
1¾ cups sugar
1   cup oil
2   cups self-rising flour

TOPPING

½   cup water
1   cup sugar

½   cup milk
1   teaspoon vanilla
1   teaspoon coconut flavoring
1   (7 ounce) can coconut

4   tablespoons butter
1   teaspoon coconut flavoring

Preheat oven to 350°. Beat eggs and sugar together. Add oil, flour, milk, vanilla and coconut flavoring. Stir in coconut. Pour into a well greased Bundt pan. Bake at 350° for 1 hour.

To make topping, combine water, sugar, butter and coconut flavoring in a small saucepan. Bring to a boil and cook 1 minute. Pour topping over baked cake while it is still warm in the pan. Cool cake before removing from pan.

Yield: 12 servings

Strawberry Daiquiri Cake

1	(18¼ ounce) package white cake mix	1	(14 ounce) can sweetened condensed milk
1	(12 ounce) can frozen strawberry daiquiri mix, thawed	1	(8 ounce) container frozen whipped topping, thawed

Bake cake in a sheet pan according to package directions. Combine daiquiri mix and milk. While still warm, poke holes in top of cake and pour daiquiri mixture over cake into holes. Use a fork to help mixture run into cake. Cool. Refrigerate until ready to serve. Spread whipped topping over cake just before serving.

Yield: 12 servings

Lemon Bundt Cake

1	(18¼ ounce) package lemon cake mix	1	cup powdered sugar
1	(3¾ ounce) package instant lemon pudding mix		Juice of 1 lemon
4	eggs	¾	cup water
2	tablespoons flour	¾	cup oil

Preheat oven to 350°. Combine cake mix, pudding mix, eggs, flour, oil and water. Pour into a lightly greased Bundt pan. Bake at 350° for 30 to 40 minutes or until a toothpick inserted in the center comes out clean. Cool cake slightly and invert onto a serving plate. Make a glaze by mixing lemon juice and sugar. Streak glaze over top of cake.

Yield: 12 servings

Italian Cream Cake

CAKE

1	stick butter
½	cup shortening
2	cups sugar
2	cups all-purpose flour
1	teaspoon baking soda

5	eggs, separated
1½	teaspoons vanilla
1	cup buttermilk
1	cup chopped nuts
1	cup flaked coconut

FROSTING

1	(16 ounce) package powdered sugar
1	(8 ounce) package cream cheese, softened

1	tablespoon vanilla
4	tablespoons butter, softened

Preheat oven to 350°. Cream butter and shortening in a large mixing bowl. Add sugar and mix well. In a separate bowl, combine flour and baking soda. Mix dry ingredients into creamed mixture. Fold in egg yolks, vanilla and buttermilk and blend until smooth. In a small bowl, beat egg whites with a mixer and fold into batter. Stir in nuts and coconut. Pour batter into two 9 inch round cake pans. Bake at 350° for 30 minutes. Cool cake before frosting.

To prepare frosting, combine sugar, cream cheese, vanilla and butter in a medium mixing bowl. Mix until creamy.

Yield: 12 to 16 servings

Believe It or Not Cake

CAKE

1	cup prunes
1½	cups sugar
1	cup oil
3	eggs
2	cups self-rising flour
1	teaspoon baking soda

ICING

1	cup sugar
½	cup buttermilk
½	teaspoon baking soda

1	teaspoon cinnamon
1	teaspoon nutmeg
1	teaspoon allspice
1	cup buttermilk
1	teaspoon vanilla
½	cup chopped pecans

1	stick butter
1	tablespoon light corn syrup
1	teaspoon vanilla

Preheat oven to 300°. Place prunes in a small saucepan and cover with water. Bring to a boil over medium heat and cook until tender. Drain and place prunes in a blender or food processor. Chop and set aside to cool. In a large mixing bowl, combine oil, sugar and eggs. Beat well. Gradually mixing in flour, baking soda, cinnamon, nutmeg and allspice. Blend until smooth. Add buttermilk and mix well. Continue to mix while adding prunes and vanilla. Stir in pecans. Pour batter into a 9x13 inch baking dish. Bake at 300° for 45 minutes.

To make icing, combine sugar, buttermilk, baking soda and butter in a medium saucepan. Cook over medium heat until butter melts. Add corn syrup and vanilla. Cook and stir until icing comes to a boil. Remove from heat and drizzle over baked cake.

Yield: 12 to 16 servings

The ingredients in this cake are hard to identify. The cake gets moister with each passing day.

Fiesta Fruit Cake

CAKE

2   cups all-purpose flour

1   (15 ounce) can crushed pineapple, undrained

2   teaspoons baking soda

1   cup chopped walnuts

2   cups sugar

2   eggs

1   teaspoon vanilla

ICING

1   (8 ounce) package light cream cheese, softened

1   stick butter, softened

1½   cups powdered sugar

1   teaspoon vanilla

    Walnuts for garnish

Preheat oven to 350°. Combine flour, pineapple, baking soda, walnuts, sugar, eggs and vanilla until blended. Pour batter into a greased 9x13 or 9x15 inch baking pan. Bake at 350° for 40 minutes.

To make icing, combine cream cheese, butter, sugar and vanilla. Spread icing over baked cake. Garnish with walnuts.

Yield: 12 to 16 servings

Paradise Delight

1	(18½ ounce) package butter flavored cake mix		2½	cups milk
1	(20 ounce) can crushed pineapple, undrained		1	(8 ounce) container frozen whipped topping, thawed
1	cup sugar		1	cup chopped nuts
1	(6 ounce) package instant vanilla pudding mix		1	(6 ounce) package shredded coconut

Prepare cake in a 9x13 inch baking pan as directed on package. In a saucepan, cook pineapple and sugar over medium heat until sugar dissolves. Poke holes in top of baked cake. Spread pineapple mixture over cake. Combine pudding mix and milk and allow to thicken slightly. Spread pudding over cake. Refrigerate cake to cool. Mix together whipped topping, nuts and coconut. Spread pudding over cake. Refrigerate until ready to serve.

Yield: 12 servings

Texas Sheet Cake a.k.a. Mississippi Mud Cake

CAKE

2	sticks butter (not margarine)
1	cup water
¼	cup cocoa
½	teaspoon salt
2	cups sugar

2	cup all-purpose flour
1	teaspoon baking soda
2	eggs
½	cup sour cream

FROSTING

1	stick butter (not margarine)
¼	cup cocoa
6	tablespoons milk

1	(16 ounce) package powdered sugar
1	teaspoon vanilla
½	cup chopped pecans, optional

Preheat oven to 400°. Melt butter in a large saucepan. Add water, cocoa and salt. Bring to a boil. Remove from heat. Stir in sugar, flour, baking soda, eggs and sour cream. Blend until smooth. Pour batter into a greased jelly-roll pan. Bake at 400° for 15 minutes; do not overbake.

Meanwhile, prepare frosting by melting butter, cocoa and milk in a medium saucepan. Remove from heat and stir in sugar, vanilla and pecans. Mix well. Apply frosting to cake while hot.

Yield: 20 servings

One Layer Chocolate Divine Cake

1	stick butter
1	(12 ounce) package milk chocolate chips
6	eggs, separated

2	teaspoons vanilla
4	tablespoons granulated sugar, divided
	Powdered sugar

Preheat oven to 350°. Microwave butter and chocolate in a microwavable bowl until melted. In a separate bowl, beat egg yolks with 1 tablespoon granulated sugar. Stir chocolate mixture and vanilla into yolks. Beat egg whites until soft peaks form. Add remaining 3 tablespoons granulated sugar to whites and beat until shiny. Fold whites into chocolate mixture. Pour batter into a springform pan. Bake at 350° for 28 minutes. Remove from oven and cover with foil to cool. Refrigerate 4 hours. Sprinkle with powdered sugar.

Yield: 8 servings

Fantastic Chocolate Chip Cake

1 (18¼ ounce) package yellow cake mix without pudding	½ cup oil
1 (3.9 ounce) package instant vanilla pudding mix	½ cup water
1 (8 ounce) container sour cream	1 (6 ounce) package chocolate chips
4 eggs, beaten	4 ounces German chocolate, grated

Preheat oven to 350°. Combine cake mix, pudding mix, sour cream, eggs, oil and water in a large bowl. Mix well. Stir in chocolates. Pour batter into a lightly greased tube or Bundt pan. Bake at 350° for 55 minutes. Remove from oven and invert onto a serving plate.

Yield: 8 to 12 servings

Classic Ultimate Cheesecake

CRUST AND FILLING

2	cups graham cracker crumbs
2	cups sugar, divided
1	stick butter or margarine, melted

7	large eggs
4	(8 ounce) packages cream cheese, cubed and softened
2	teaspoons vanilla

TOPPING

1	(16 ounce) container sour cream
½	cup sugar

⅛	teaspoon vanilla

Stir together crumbs, ¼ cup sugar and butter. Press mixture into bottom and 1 inch up sides of a 10 inch springform pan. Chill crust 1 hour. Preheat oven to 350°. Beat eggs with an electric mixer at medium speed. Add cream cheese and beat until blended. Gradually beat in remaining 1¾ cups sugar. Stir in vanilla. Pour batter into chilled crust. Bake at 350° for 1 hour, 15 minutes. Cool on a wire rack for 10 minutes while increasing oven temperature to 425°. Prepare topping by combining sour cream, sugar and vanilla. Spread topping over cheesecake. Bake at 425° for 5 to 7 minutes. Cool on rack for 1 hour. Cover and chill at least 10 minutes.

Yield: 8 to 12 servings

Caramel Brownie Cheesecake

1¾ cups vanilla wafer crumbs	1 cup brown sugar
5 tablespoons butter, melted	3 large eggs
1 (14 ounce) package caramels	1 (8 ounce) container sour cream
1 (5 ounce) can evaporated milk	2 teaspoons vanilla
2 cups boxed dry brownie mix (no frosting)	Whipped cream
3 (8 ounce) packages cream cheese, cubed and softened	

Preheat oven to 350°. Combine crumbs and butter. Stir well and press firmly into the bottom and 2 inches up the sides of a 9 inch springform pan. Bake at 350° for 5 minutes. Cool on a wire rack. Combine caramels and milk in a small heavy saucepan. Cook over low heat, stirring often, until caramels melt. Pour mixture over crust. Sprinkle brownie mix on top. In a mixing bowl, beat cream cheese with an electric mixer on medium speed for 2 minutes. Gradually beat in sugar. Add eggs, one at a time, beating well after each addition. Stir in sour cream and vanilla. Pour batter over brownie mix. Bake at 350° for 50 to 60 minutes or until set. Cool to room temperature. Cover and chill at least 4 hours. Remove sides of pan. Garnish with whipped cream.

Yield: 8 to 10 servings

Kahlúa Chocolate Cheesecake

½	(20 ounce) package double filling chocolate sandwich cookies, crushed		2	large eggs, beaten
1½	cups semi-sweet chocolate chips		⅓	cup granulated sugar
¼	cup Kahlúa		¼	teaspoon salt
2	tablespoons butter		1	cup sour cream
			2	(8 ounce) packages cream cheese

Preheat oven to 350°. Press crushed cookies into a 10 inch springform pan. Heat chocolate chips, Kahlúa and butter in a saucepan over medium heat until melted. Stir until smooth. In a mixing bowl, beat eggs, sugar, salt, sour cream and cream cheese together until smooth. Gradually beat chocolate mixture into cream cheese mixture. Pour batter into pan. Bake at 350° for 40 minutes or just until center is set. Remove from oven and let stand 1 hour. Refrigerate overnight.

Yield: 12 to 14 servings

Frozen Mocha Mousse Cheesecake

1¼ cups chocolate wafer crumbs (about 24 wafers), plus extra for garnish
¼ cup sugar
4 tablespoons butter, melted
1 (8 ounce) package cream cheese, cubed and softened
1 (14 ounce) can sweetened condensed milk
⅔ cup chocolate syrup
2 tablespoons instant coffee
1 teaspoon hot water
1 cup heavy cream, whipped

Combine crumbs, sugar and butter in a small bowl. Mix well and press into the bottom and 1 inch up sides of a greased 9 inch springform pan or a 9x13 inch baking dish. Chill. In a large bowl, beat cream cheese until fluffy. Add milk and syrup. In a cup, dissolve coffee in hot water and add to cream cheese mixture. Blend well. Fold in whipped cream. Pour into pan and cover. Freeze 6 to 7 hours or until firm. Garnish with extra crumbs.

Yield: 8 to 12 servings

New England Style Bananas Foster

⅓ cup maple syrup
⅓ cup dark rum
3½ cups diagonally sliced firm bananas
⅓ cup chopped walnuts, toasted
3 cups vanilla ice cream

Combine syrup and rum in a large nonstick skillet. Bring to a simmer over medium-low heat. Add bananas and cook 3 minutes, stirring occasionally. Add walnuts and cook 1 minute. Serve immediately over ice cream.

Yield: 6 servings

Strawberry Layered Dessert

2	cups self-rising flour	3	cups powdered sugar	
2	sticks butter, melted	1	(21 ounce) can strawberry pie filling, chilled	
2	cups chopped pecans	3	cups sliced fresh strawberries, or 2 (10 ounce) containers frozen, drained, chilled	
1	(8 ounce) package cream cheese			
1	(16 ounce) container frozen whipped topping, thawed			

Preheat oven to 300°. Combine flour, butter and pecans and press into a 9x13 inch pan. Bake at 300° for 20 to 25 minutes. Cool crust completely. Mix together cream cheese, whipped topping and sugar and spread over crust. Combine pie filling and strawberries and spread over cream cheese layer.

Yield: 12 to 14 servings

Anytime Banana Pudding

2	(3.9 ounce) packages instant banana pudding mix	1	(16 ounce) container frozen whipped topping, thawed	
3	cups cold milk	1	(14 ounce) package coconut cookie bars	
1	(14 ounce) can sweetened condensed milk	6	bananas, sliced	

Combine pudding mix and cold milk in a large bowl. Fold in whipped topping. Mix in condensed milk. Arrange a layer of cookie bars in a large glass bowl. Add a layer of bananas and a layer of pudding mixture. Repeat layers until pudding is final layer on top. Sprinkle with any cookie crumbs from package. Chill and serve.

Yield: 16 servings

Mama T's Dessert

CRUST

1½ sticks butter, melted
1 cup chopped pecans

1½ cups all-purpose flour

FILLING LAYERS AND TOPPING

1 cup powdered sugar
1 (8 ounce) container frozen whipped topping, thawed, divided
1 (8 ounce) package cream cheese, cubed and softened

2 (3.9 ounce) packages instant chocolate pudding mix
3 cups cold milk
4 (1.4 ounce) English toffee candy bars, chopped

Preheat oven to 350˚. Combine butter, pecans and flour and press into a 9x13 inch pan. Bake at 350˚ for 30 minutes. Cool.

To make first filling layer, blend sugar, 1 cup whipped topping and cream cheese. Spread over cooled crust. Prepare second layer by combining pudding mix and milk. Allow to thicken and then spread over first layer. Top with remaining whipped topping and sprinkle with candy. Refrigerate until ready to serve.

Yield: 12 to 16 servings

For a slightly different variation, make the following changes:

Crush 1 (16 ounce) package chocolate sandwich cookies, reserving 1 cup for topping. Combine remaining cookie crumbs with 1½ sticks butter to make a crust. Do not bake.

The first filling layer does not change. For the second filling layer, use chocolate or vanilla pudding mix.

For the topping, sprinkle reserved cookie crumbs over whipped topping instead of candy. Now you have made a Black Cow!

Yield: 12 to 16 servings

I Want "s'More" Eclair Squares

2	(3.9 ounce) packages instant French vanilla pudding mix	3	tablespoons butter
3	cups milk	1	tablespoon vanilla
1	(8 ounce) container frozen whipped topping, thawed	1½	cups powdered sugar
2	(1 ounce) squares unsweetened chocolate	2	sleeves graham crackers

Combine pudding mix, milk and whipped topping; set aside. In a saucepan, melt chocolate and butter until smooth. Remove from heat and stir in vanilla and sugar. In a 4½ x10 inch pan, layer graham crackers and half the pudding mixture. Repeat layers. Add another layer of graham crackers. Top with chocolate mixture. Refrigerate overnight before serving.

Yield: 12 servings

Strawberry Trifle

1	(6 ounce) package instant vanilla pudding mix	1	(8 ounce) container frozen whipped topping, thawed
1	prepared angel food cake		Sliced almonds
1	(16 ounce) package frozen strawberries		

Prepare pudding according to package directions. Break cake into small pieces. Layer half the cake pieces, half the strawberries, half the pudding and half the whipped topping in a trifle dish. Repeat layers in same order. Garnish with almonds.

Yield: 8 to 12 servings

Sweet Dreams Chocolate Trifle

1 **(16 ounce) package fudge brownie mix**
½ **cup Kahlúa**
3 **(3.9 ounce) packages instant chocolate pudding mix**

1 **(16 ounce) container frozen whipped topping, thawed, divided**
3 **(1.4 ounce) English toffee candy bars, crushed**

Prepare brownie mix and bake in a 9x13 inch baking pan according to package directions. Poke top of warm brownies in 1 inch intervals with a fork. Drizzle Kahlúa over the top. Cool, then crumble brownies. Prepare pudding mix according to package directions. Do not chill. Place a third of crumbled brownies in the bottom of a 3 quart trifle dish or large glass bowl. Top with a third of pudding and a third of whipped topping. Sprinkle a third of candy bar over top. Repeat layers 2 times with remaining ingredients. Chill 8 hours before serving.

Yield: 8 to 12 servings

Kahlúa can be omitted, or substitute ¼ cup strong coffee mixed with 1 teaspoon sugar, if desired.

Amaretto Ice Cream Dessert

8	**large ice cream sandwiches**	**3**	**(1.4 ounce) English toffee candy bars, chopped**
⅓	**cup amaretto**	**2**	**(1.5 ounce) chocolate candy bars, shaved**
1	**(16 ounce) container frozen whipped topping, thawed, divided**		

Place ice cream sandwiches in a 9x13 inch glass baking dish. Drizzle amaretto over top. Spread half of whipped topping over sandwiches and sprinkle with English toffee candy bars. Spread remaining whipped topping over candy. Garnish with shaved chocolate bars. Freeze and enjoy this great summer dessert.

Yield: 8 servings

Club House Specialties: Beverages to Whet your Whistles

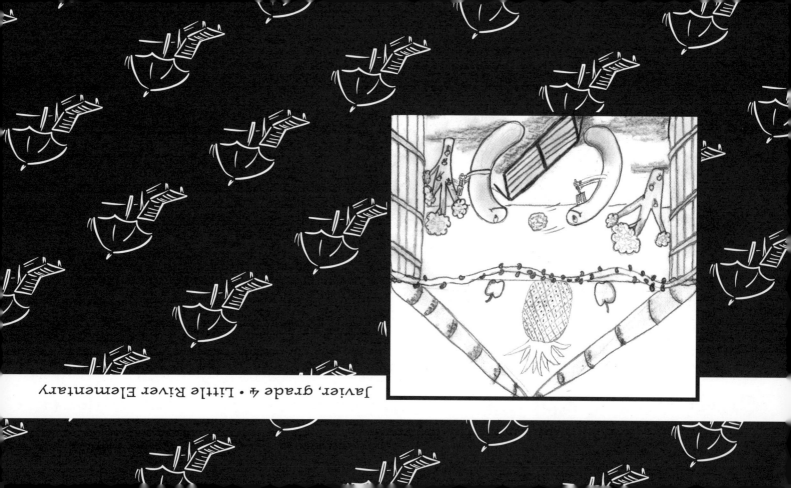

Javier, grade 4 • Little River Elementary

Tutti Fruity Punch

3   quarts pineapple juice
1½ cups lemon juice
3   cups orange juice
⅓   cup lime juice
2½ cups sugar

1   cup slightly crushed fresh mint leaves
4   (12 ounce) containers ginger ale
2   (12 ounce) containers carbonated water
1   pint fresh strawberries, sliced
    Ice or ice ring, preferably made with fruit juice

Combine juices. Stir in sugar and mint. Chill. Just before serving, add ginger ale, carbonated water and strawberries. Add ice or ice ring, or serve over ice.

Yield: 30 servings

Banana Fruit Punch

3½ cups sugar
6   cups water
3   cups pineapple juice
2   cups orange juice

    Juice of 2 lemons
3   large bananas, mashed
2   (28 ounce) bottles ginger ale

Combine sugar, water, juices and bananas in a large bowl. Freeze in a covered container for 24 hours. When ready to serve, thaw at room temperature for 45 minutes. Pour ginger ale over mixture or spoon mixture into glasses and pour ginger ale on top.

Yield: 25 servings

Laura's Brunch Punch

1	(46 ounce) can pineapple juice
3	(.13 ounce) packages dry unsweetened pink lemonade drink mix
1	cup sugar
1	(1 liter) bottle lemon-lime soda
1	large bag ice

Combine juice, drink mix, sugar, soda and ice in a large bowl. Serve.

Yield: 12 servings

Refreshing Punch

1	gallon apple cider
2	(6 ounce) cans frozen lemonade concentrate
6	ounces bottled lemon juice
2	quarts ginger ale

Combine cider, lemonade concentrate and lemon juice in a bowl. Stir in ginger ale. Chill and serve very cold.

Yield: 25 servings

Sparkling Grape Lemonade

1   cup unsweetened white grape juice, chilled
½ cup frozen lemonade concentrate, thawed

2½ cups club soda, chilled
    Lemon zest curls, optional

Combine juice and lemonade concentrate in a pitcher. Stir in club soda just before serving. Serve over ice. Garnish each serving with lemon zest.

Yield: 4 servings

Summer Sangría

1   (750 ml) bottle white wine, chilled
1   (750 ml) bottle Merlot, chilled
1   (32 ounce) bottle cranberry peach juice, chilled
1   cup fresh orange juice
1   cup brandy

2   cinnamon sticks or ½ teaspoon ground cinnamon
2   oranges, divided
2   limes, divided
1   (12 ounce) can lemon-lime soda

Combine wines, juices and brandy in a large container. Slice one orange and one lime and add to sangría mixture. Stir in cinnamon and chill. When ready to serve, stir in soda. Slice remaining orange and cut remaining lime into wedges. Serve sangría over ice in tumblers. Garnish each serving with an orange slice and lime wedge.

Yield: 12 or more servings

Without soda, sangría mixture will keep for several days in refrigerator. To prepare by the glass, use three-fourths sangría mixture to one-fourth soda.

Creamy Coffee Punch

4	quarts strong cold coffee	1	cup sugar
1	quart cold milk	2	quarts vanilla ice cream
1	tablespoon vanilla		

Combine coffee, milk and vanilla in a large container. Stir in sugar until dissolved. Chill thoroughly. When ready to serve, pour mixture over ice cream in a punch bowl.

Yield: about 30 (punch cup size) servings

Hot Spiced Tea

1	cup Tang	½	teaspoon cinnamon
½	cup sugar	½	teaspoon ground cloves
1	(6 ounce) package sweetened dry lemonade mix		
¼	cup instant tea		

Combine all ingredients in an airtight jar. To serve, add 3 to 4 teaspoons of mixture to a glass. Add 1 cup hot water or as much water to suit taste.

Yield: 1 quart dry mix

Party Piña Colada Slush

1 **(46 ounce) can pineapple juice**	2 **cups light rum**
2 **(12 ounce) cans frozen lemonade concentrate, thawed**	1 **(15 ounce) can cream of coconut**
3 **cups water**	1 **(2 liter) bottle lemon-lime soda, chilled**

Combine juice, lemonade concentrate, water, rum and cream of coconut in a large plastic container. Freeze at least 8 hours, stirring twice during the freezing process. To serve, combine equal portions of frozen mixture and soda. Stir well and serve immediately. Store any remaining mixture in freezer.

Yield: 6 quarts

This recipe works great served in a punch bowl.

Tropical Delight

3 **tablespoons dark rum**	2 **tablespoons cream of coconut**
2 **tablespoons pineapple juice**	1 **cup ice**
2 **tablespoons orange juice**	1 **tablespoon orange liqueur**

In a blender, process rum, juices and cream of coconut. Pour mixture over ice in a glass. Top with liqueur. Garnish with kiwi slices or cherries.

Yield: 1 serving

Frozen Margarita Punch

4	(12 ounce) cans frozen limeade concentrate, thawed		3	quarts water
3	cups tequila		3	cups triple sec
2	(2 liter) bottles lemon-lime soda			
1	lime, sliced			

Combine limeade concentrate, water, triple sec and tequila in 2 quart freezer containers. Freeze overnight, stirring at least twice during the freezing process. Remove from freezer 30 minutes before serving. When ready to serve, break into chunks in a punch bowl or large container. Add soda and stir until mixture is slushy. Garnish by floating lime slices on top.

Yield: 12 to 24 servings

Vodka Freeze

1	(6 ounce) can frozen orange juice concentrate, thawed		3½	cups water
1	(12 ounce) can frozen lemonade concentrate, thawed		2	cups vodka
2	(6 ounce) cans frozen limeade concentrate, thawed		2	(2 liter) bottles lemon-lime soda
⅓	cup sugar			

Combine orange juice, concentrates, sugar, water and vodka. Freeze. To serve, combine equal amounts of slush mixture and soda in glasses.

Yield: 12 to 24 servings

Brandy Slush

4	orange spice tea bags	1	(12 ounce) can frozen orange juice concentrate
2	cups boiling water	1	(12 ounce) can frozen lemonade concentrate
2	cups sugar	1	pint apricot brandy
7	cups water, divided		Lemon-lime soda

Combine tea bags and boiling water and let steep for 10 minutes. In a saucepan, combine sugar and 2 cups water. Bring to a boil and cook until sugar dissolves. Remove from heat and stir in remaining 5 cups water, concentrates and brandy. Add steeped tea and mix. Pour into a large plastic container and freeze. To serve, spoon frozen mixture into tall glasses and add soda.

Yield: 12 to 24 servings

This is a great holiday recipe.

For a Bourbon Slush, use plain tea bags instead of the orange spice variety and substitute 1 pint bourbon for the apricot brandy.

Cosmopolitan Martini

1	ounce vodka	¼	ounce lime juice
¼	ounce triple sec	1½	ounces cranberry juice

Combine vodka, triple sec and juices in a cocktail shaker filled with crushed ice. Shake quickly until shaker is ice cold. Strain mixture into a chilled martini glass. Garnish with lime zest curls.

Yield: 1 serving

Cookie Express

1¼ cups brandy		**2-3 chocolate sandwich cookies**	
¾ cup dark crème de cacao		**Vanilla ice cream to taste**	

Combine brandy, creme de cacao, cookies and ice cream in a blender. Process until thoroughly mixed. Serve immediately.

Yield: 4 servings

Cheap brandy tastes best in this recipe.

West Indies Yellowbird

1 ounce Galliano liqueur		**¼ cup pineapple juice**	
1½ ounces light rum		**¼ cup orange juice**	
¼ ounce crème de banane			

Combine liqueur, rum, creme de banana and juices and mix well. Pour into a tall glass over ice. Garnish with orange slices or cherries.

Yield: 1 serving

Playground Favorites: Sure to Delight Kids of All Ages

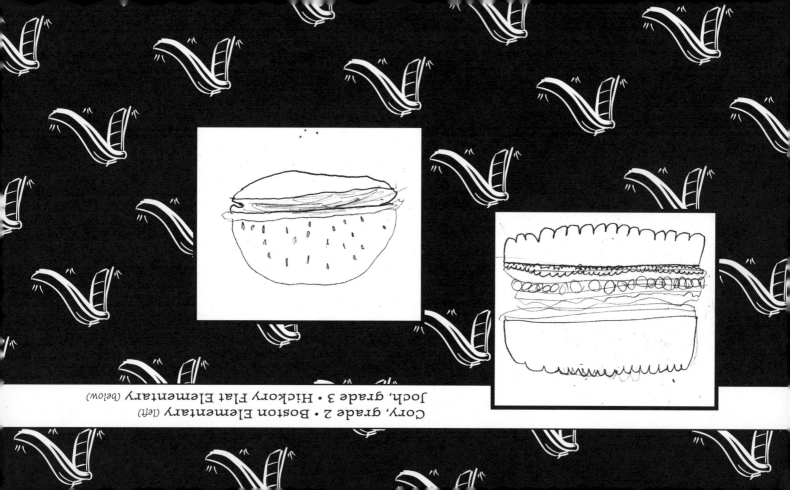

Cory, grade 2 • Boston Elementary (left)
Josh, grade 3 • Hickory Flat Elementary (below)

Delicious Lemonade

Juice of 4 lemons
Juice of 1 orange
2   cups bottled lemon juice

3   cups sugar
1   (2 liter) bottle lemon-lime soda
2   liters water

Combine juices, sugar, soda and water in a large bowl. Serve over ice.

Yield: 1 gallon plus

Orange Jubilee

1   (6 ounce) can frozen orange juice concentrate
½   cup evaporated milk
½   cup water

¼   cup sugar
½   teaspoon vanilla
5-6   ice cubes

Combine concentrate, milk, water, sugar, vanilla and ice in a blender. Process 30 seconds or until smooth.

Yield: 2 servings

Grandma's Caramel Corn

4	sticks butter	½	teaspoon baking soda
½	cup light corn syrup	1	teaspoon vanilla
1	teaspoon salt	6	quarts popped popcorn (2 cups unpopped)

Preheat oven to 250°. Melt butter in a saucepan. Add corn syrup and salt and bring to a boil. Boil slowly for 5 minutes without stirring. Immediately add baking soda and vanilla. Pour mixture over popcorn in a large greased roasting pan. Mix well. Bake at 250° for 1 hour, stirring every 15 minutes. Store in an airtight container.

Yield: 6 quarts

Peanuts or M&M's can be added to prepared caramel corn.

Oreo Milk Shake

1	pint chocolate or vanilla ice cream	8	chocolate sandwich cookies
¾	cup milk		Whipped cream

Combine ice cream and milk in a blender. Process until smooth. Add cookies and blend just until mixed through. Top individual servings with whipped cream.

Yield: 2 (8 ounce) servings

Muddy Buddies

9   cups Chex cereal, any variety
1   cup semi-sweet chocolate chips
½   cup peanut butter

4   tablespoons margarine or butter
1   teaspoon vanilla
1½ cups powdered sugar

Place cereal in a large bowl; set aside. Microwave chocolate, peanut butter and margarine in an uncovered 1 quart microwavable bowl on high for 1 minute. Stir. Microwave 30 seconds longer or until melted and smooth when stirred. Mix in vanilla. Pour mixture over cereal in bowl. Stir until evenly coated. Pour into a large plastic zip-top bag. Add powdered sugar. Seal bag and shake until well coated. Spread on wax paper to cool. Store in an airtight container in the refrigerator.

Yield: 9 cups

Graham Crackers

1   stick butter
1   stick margarine
½   cup sugar

1   (1 pound) box honey graham crackers
1   (2 ounce) package sliced almonds

Preheat oven to 325°. Melt butter, margarine and sugar together in a small saucepan over medium to low heat. Bring to a boil and cook 2 minutes. Line two jelly roll pans with parchment paper. Place a single layer of graham crackers over the parchment paper. Pour butter mixture over crackers. Sprinkle almonds on top. Bake at 325° for 10 minutes. Do not overbake or crackers will get too hard. Remove from oven and cool. Cut cooled crackers along perforations into quarters.

Yield: about 150 quarter pieces

Monkey Bread

4	(10 ounce) cans refrigerated biscuits	1½	cups brown sugar
1	tablespoon cinnamon	1½	sticks butter

Preheat oven to 350°. Cut each biscuit into quarters. Combine sugar and cinnamon in a bowl. Roll biscuit pieces in mixture, reserving any remaining mixture, melt butter with remaining sugar mixture. Place half of the biscuits in a greased Bundt pan. Pour half the butter mixture over the biscuits. Repeat with remaining ingredients. Bake at 350° for 30 to 35 minutes.

Yield: 12 to 16 servings

For variety, mix ½ cup chopped pecans or raisins with ¼ cup sugar and 1 teaspoon cinnamon and add to pan with biscuit pieces.

Rudolph Reindeer Cookies

1	(18 ounce) can refrigerator slice and bake sugar or peanut butter cookie dough	1	(10 ounce) package red and green M&M's
		1	(10 ounce) bag mini bow pretzels

Slice dough as directed on package. Place slices on an ungreased baking sheet and pinch in sides slightly so cookies resemble animal heads. Place a red M&M for a nose, 2 green M&M's for eyes and 2 pretzels for antlers. Bake as directed on dough package.

Yield: 17 cookies

Monster Cookies

1	dozen eggs		4	sticks butter, softened
2	pounds brown sugar		3	pounds crunchy peanut butter
4	cups granulated sugar		18	cups oatmeal
1	tablespoon vanilla		1	pound chocolate chips
2	tablespoons plus 2 teaspoons baking soda		1	pound M&M's

Preheat oven to 350°. Combine eggs, sugars, vanilla, baking soda and butter with a mixer. By hand, stir in peanut butter, oatmeal, chocolate chips and M&M's. Use a small ice cream scoop to spoon cookies onto ungreased baking sheets, 6 cookies per sheet. Bake at 350° for 20 minutes.

Yield: 9 dozen

Cookie dough may be wrapped in plastic and foil and frozen until ready to bake.

Florida Snowball Cookies

1	(12 ounce) package vanilla wafers	¾	cup shredded coconut
½	cup frozen orange juice concentrate, thawed	½	cup chopped pecans
1¾	cups powdered sugar, divided		

Crush wafers into crumbs by placing wafers in a plastic zip-top bag and rolling with a rolling pin. Place wafer crumbs in a large mixing bowl. Add juice concentrate, ¾ cup powdered sugar, coconut and pecans. Mix well. Roll mixture into 1 inch diameter balls. Roll each ball in remaining 1 cup powdered sugar. Store in an airtight container, separating cookies with wax paper. No baking involved.

Yield: about 4 to 5 dozen

Haystacks

2	cups sugar	2½	cups dry oats
½	cup milk	½	cup peanut butter
¼	cup cocoa	1	teaspoon vanilla
1	stick butter		

Combine sugar, milk, cocoa and butter in a large saucepan. Bring to a boil and cook 1 minute. Remove from heat and stir in oats, peanut butter and vanilla. Mix well. Pour into a well-greased 9x13 inch pan. Chill until firm. Cut into small squares.

Yield: 24 servings

Snickerdoodles

1¾ cups sugar, divided
1 stick butter, softened
½ cup shortening
2 eggs
2¾ cups all-purpose flour

2 teaspoons cream of tartar
1 teaspoon baking soda
¼ teaspoon salt
2 teaspoons cinnamon

Preheat oven to 350°. In a large bowl, cream 1½ cups sugar, butter, shortening and eggs together using an electric mixer. In a separate bowl, combine flour, cream of tartar, baking soda and salt. Gradually beat dry ingredients into sugar mixture with mixer. In a small dish, combine remaining ¼ cup sugar and cinnamon. Shape dough into balls. Roll each ball in cinnamon sugar mixture. Place balls 2 inches apart on an ungreased baking sheet. Bake at 350° for 8 to 10 minutes or until set. Remove from baking sheet and cool on a wire rack.

Yield: 3 dozen

Gooey Turtle Bars

2	**cups graham cracker crumbs**		
1	**stick butter or margarine, melted**	**1**	**(12 ounce) jar caramel topping**
2	**cups semi-sweet chocolate chips (12 ounces)**	**1**	**cup pecan pieces**

Preheat oven to 350°. Combine crumbs and butter in an ungreased 9x13 inch pan. Stir until mixed and press firmly into bottom of pan. Sprinkle with chocolate chips and pecans. Remove jar lid and microwave caramel topping for 1 minute on high. Drizzle topping over chocolate and pecans. Bake at 350° for 15 minutes. Cool in pan. Chill at least 30 minutes before cutting into bars.

Yield: 20 to 24 servings

Magic Bars

1	**stick butter**	**1**	**(14 ounce) can sweetened condensed milk**
1½	**cups graham cracker crumbs**	**1**	**(6 ounce) package semi-sweet chocolate chips**
		1⅓	**cups flaked coconut**
		1	**cup chopped nuts**

Preheat oven to 350°. (Use 325° for a glass pan.) Place butter in a 9x13 inch baking pan. Melt butter in oven. Sprinkle crumbs over butter and press into pan with a spoon. Pour milk over crumbs. Top with chocolate chips, coconut and nuts. Press down firmly. Bake at 350° for 25 to 30 minutes or until lightly browned. Cool before cutting.

Yield: 2 dozen

Cereal Peanut Bars

½ cup light corn syrup
¼ cup brown sugar
  Dash of salt
1 cup peanut butter

1 teaspoon vanilla
2 cups crispy rice cereal
1½ cups corn flakes cereal
1 cup chocolate chips

Combine corn syrup, sugar and salt in a saucepan. Bring to a boil. Stir in peanut butter. Remove from heat and stir in vanilla. Mix in cereals and chocolate chips. Press mixture into a greased 9 inch square pan. Cover and chill 1 hour before cutting into bars.

Yield: 12 bars

Lemonade Stand Pie

1 (6 ounce) can frozen lemonade concentrate, partially thawed
1 pint vanilla ice cream, softened

1 (8 ounce) container frozen whipped topping, thawed
1 (6 ounce) graham cracker crust

Use an electric mixer to beat lemonade concentrate on low for 30 seconds. Gradually spoon in ice cream, beating until well blended. Stir in whipped topping until smooth. Spoon mixture into crust; if needed, freeze mixture until thick enough to spoon into crust. Freeze pie for 4 hours or until firm. Let stand at room temperature for 30 minutes before serving.

Yield: 8 servings

Banana Split Cake

Yield: 12 servings

3½	sticks margarine, divided
3	cups graham cracker crumbs
1	(20 ounce) can crushed pineapple, drained, juice reserved
2	cups powdered sugar
5	bananas
1	(16 ounce) container frozen whipped topping, thawed
1	cup chopped nuts
	Halved maraschino cherries

Melt 1½ sticks margarine and combine with cracker crumbs. Press mixture into a 9x13 inch pan. Combine remaining 2 sticks margarine, softened, with pineapple and powdered sugar. Beat with an electric mixer on medium speed for 15 minutes. Spread mixture over cracker crust. Slice bananas into reserved pineapple juice. Drain juice and place banana slices on top of cake. Top with whipped topping, nuts and cherries. Refrigerate overnight for best results.

No Bake Chocolate Chip Cookie Pie

Yield: 8 servings

1	(15 ounce) package chocolate chip cookies, divided
1	cup milk
1	(9 ounce) graham cracker crust
1	(8 ounce) container frozen whipped topping, thawed, divided

Dip 8 cookies in milk and place in a single layer in crust. Top with one-third of whipped topping. Repeat layers with 8 more milk-dipped cookies and remaining whipped topping. Crumble 2 cookies over top. Cover and chill 8 hours.

Dirt Pudding Dessert

1	(16 ounce) package chocolate sandwich cookies		3½	cups milk
4	tablespoons butter, softened		2	(3.9 ounce) boxes vanilla instant pudding
1	(8 ounce) package cream cheese, softened		1	(12 ounce) container frozen whipped topping, thawed
1	cup powdered sugar			

Grind cookies in a food processor or blender or crush in a plastic bag with a rolling pin to make crumbs; set aside. In a mixing bowl, cream butter, cream cheese and sugar together. In a separate bowl, mix milk and pudding. Gently fold in whipped topping. Stir pudding mixture into creamed mixture. Place one-third of cookie crumbs into a clean 8 inch plastic flowerpot. Layer half of the pudding and half of the remaining crumbs on top. Repeat layers, ending with crumbs. Chill 8 hours or overnight.

Yield: 1 (8-inch) flowerpot or 2 smaller pots

Decorate pot with artificial flowers. Serve dessert with a garden trowel. Add a few gummy worms between layers and on top as a garnish.

Homemade Vanilla Ice Cream

2	(¼ ounce) packages unflavored gelatin		2	cups sugar
1	cup cool water		2	teaspoons vanilla
3	eggs, divided			Pinch of salt
9	cups milk		1	cup sweet cream, whipped

Dissolve unflavored gelatin in one cup of cool water and set aside. Beat egg yolks and combine with milk in large sauce pan. Heat milk mixture until warm, but do not boil. Remove from heat and add dissolved gelatin, sugar, vanilla, salt and stiffly beaten egg whites. Let cool, then add whipped sweet cream. Pour into a prepared ice cream machine and process until frozen.

Yield: About 1 gallon, 12 servings

A

Home Court Advantage

Junior Service League of Woodstock
P.O. Box 1672
Woodstock, GA 30188
(770) 592-3535

Please send me_____copies of Home Court Advantage   @ $15.00 each (price includes tax) $ _____

Add postage and handling   @ $ 4.00 each $ _____

Total Enclosed $ _____

Please make checks payable to Junior Service League of Woodstock.
Allow 3–4 weeks for delivery.

Name _____

Address _____

City _____ State _____ Zip _____